English World

Student's Book 9 B1+

 International House London
16 Stukeley Street, Covent Garden
London WC2B 5LQ
Main Tel: +44 (0) 20 7611 2400
Fax: +44 (0) 20 7117 4175
Web site: www.ihlondon.com

Mary Bowen, Liz Hocking & Wendy Wren

Unit	Reading	Reading comprehension	Grammar	Word focus
1￼An international school￼Page 6	*Persuasion*￼advertisements	literal questions;￼definitions;￼discussion of advertising;￼opinions;￼personal response	modal verbs + passive infinitive￼*The forest might be cleared.*￼*Can the planet be saved?*	**Dictionary work:** headwords￼**Spelling:** *ou*￼**Word groups:** festival and forest￼**Prefixes:** *de- / dis- / af- / re- / in-*
2￼Music￼Page 16	*Classical is best!*￼an email discussing an issue	literal questions;￼phrase definitions;￼discussion of style;￼discussion of content;￼personal response	reported questions￼tense shifting: present → past; past → past perfect;￼*will* → *would*￼"Is the boy ill?" → *They asked if the boy was ill.*	**Dictionary work:** words with two or more meanings (1)￼**Spelling:** /uː/￼**Word groups:** positive and negative adjectives￼**Prefixes:** *inter-*
Study skills 1	Paragraphs			
3￼It's a mystery …￼Page 28	*Z for Zachariah*￼a story with an unusual opening	literal questions;￼defining words / expressions;￼inferential questions about story openings;￼personal response	participle clauses￼*Arriving at the station, John bought a ticket.*￼*Damaged by the storm, the boat sank.*	**Dictionary work:** words with two or more meanings (2)￼**Spelling:** /eɪ/￼**Word groups:** time and weather￼**Prefixes:** *bi- / tele-*
4￼It's a fact!￼Page 38	*Sharing the Planet: Animals in Science*￼a television documentary review	literal questions;￼phrase definitions;￼inferential questions;￼personal response;￼reviews	non-defining relative clauses￼*We met Mario, who is a famous opera singer.*￼*Tigers, which were once common, are now rare.*	**Dictionary work:** words with two or more meanings (3)￼**Spelling:** long o￼**Word groups:** television￼**Suffixes:** *-ology / ist*
Life skills 1	Filling in forms			
5￼There's a problem￼Page 50	*Champion*￼a play script in two scenes	identifying speakers;￼discussion of character, structure, content;￼personal response	*to be able to*: (all tenses)￼*I was able to swim when I was four.*￼*I haven't been able to sleep.*	**Dictionary work:** example phrases / sentences￼**Spelling:** /ɪ/￼**Word groups:** sport￼**Suffixes:** *-ment / -ness / -ship / -dom*
6￼Sounds amazing – let's go!￼Page 60	*Istanbul – a city of two continents*￼a travelogue from a magazine	literal questions;￼phrase definitions;￼inferential questions;￼personal response	future perfect simple￼*By the time you read this letter, I will have left the country.*	**Dictionary work:** grammar boxes￼**Spelling:** *-le / -el / -al* endings￼**Word groups:** buildings and transport￼**Prefixes:** *ir-*
Study skills 2	Research			
7￼It's a classic￼Page 72	*A New Year Ball*￼an extract from a classic novel	identifying speakers;￼discussion of characters;￼phrase definitions;￼inferential questions;￼personal response	the indirect object as the subject of a passive sentence￼*He was sent an email.*￼*She was given a present by her uncle.*	**Dictionary work:** Build Your Vocabulary boxes￼**Spelling:** plurals with *-s* and *-es*￼**Word groups:** things people wear￼**Suffixes:** *-ic*
8￼Finding out￼Page 82	*Human achievement – spaceflight*￼an article giving information and explanations	literal questions;￼sequencing;￼inferential questions;￼discussion of issues;￼personal response	future perfect passive￼*By the end of the century, many new discoveries will have been made.*	**Dictionary work:** subject labels￼**Spelling:** plurals of words ending in *-y*￼**Word groups:** specialised subjects￼**Prefixes:** *re-*
Life skills 2	Formal letter writing			
9￼It's an issue￼Page 94	*The Age of the Automobile*￼a discursive essay	literal questions;￼phrase definitions;￼questions about discursive style;￼inferential questions;￼personal response	reported speech: changes to *this*, *these*, *here* and adverbs of time￼"I saw this film last year."￼*He said that he had seen that film the year before.*	**Dictionary work:** bold words in the definition￼**Spelling:** plurals of words ending in *-f / -fe*￼**Word groups:** specialised subjects￼**Suffixes:** *-ed / -d / -t*
10￼Influences￼Page 104	*Leo*￼an autobiographical extract about an important person in the writer's life	literal questions;￼phrase definitions;￼scanning for detail;￼inferential questions;￼personal response	*would* + infinitive (without *to*) to express habitual actions in the past￼*During the holidays we would camp on the beach.*	**Dictionary work:** synonyms and antonyms￼**Spelling:** disappearing letters￼**Word groups:** word classes￼**Suffixes:** *-ive*
Study skills 3	Revision		Projects Page 116	

Grammar in use	Listening and speaking	Writing features
question tags (all tenses) *They went abroad, didn't they?* *He will phone, won't he?*	**Listening comprehension:** matching advertisements to products **Individual speaking:** advertisements	persuasive writing SB: features and assignment – creating an advertisement WB: planning sheet
transitive and intransitive phrasal verbs *He made up a story.* *The thief made off.*	**Functions of English:** asking for and giving opinions **Listening comprehension:** answering questions on a dialogue	discursive writing SB: features and assignment – How much should pupils be involved in running their school? WB: planning sheet
modal verbs + perfect infinitive *You should have locked the door.* *He might have lost his mobile.*	**Listening comprehension:** dialogue: completing a chart **Individual speaking:** organising an event	story openings SB: features and assignment – an unusual story opening WB: planning sheet
third conditional *If you had seen the film, you would have enjoyed it.* *I would have phoned if I had had your number.*	**Functions of English:** agreeing and disagreeing **Listening comprehension:** dialogue: Are facts true, false or not stated?	a review SB: features and assignment – a television documentary WB: planning sheet
reported questions with modal verbs *"Must we leave?"* *He asked if they had to leave.*	**Listening comprehension:** monologue: a talk about an artist: multiple choice questions **Individual speaking:** an artist from your country	writing about issues SB: features and assignment – completing the play script WB: planning sheet
relative clauses with *whose*; defining and non-defining relative clauses *That's the man whose car was stolen.*	**Functions of English:** offering to do something; accepting or refusing an offer of help **Listening comprehension:** short dialogues: mutiple choice and literal questions	a travelogue SB: features and assignment – a town or city you know well WB: planning sheet
pronouns (subject, direct object, indirect object, possessive); possessive adjectives	**Listening comprehension:** dialogue: Are facts true, false or not stated? **Individual speaking:** your favourite author	narrative extract SB: features and assignment – character preparing for new experience WB: planning sheet
separable and inseparable phrasal verbs *I filled in the form. I filled the form in. I filled it in.* *He looked after the boys. He looked after them.*	**Functions of English:** making requests **Listening comprehension:** answering questions on a dialogue	informing and explaining SB: features and assignment – hot-air balloon or shuttle landing WB: planning sheet
the order of adjectives before nouns *She wore a beautiful, old, red, Indian, silk shawl.*	**Listening comprehension:** monologue: a talk about archaeology and art: Are the facts true, false or not stated? **Individual speaking:** an interesting discovery	discursive essay SB: features and assignment – fashion or computer games WB: planning sheet
causatives with *have* and *get* *Jane had her photo taken.* *Bob got the car fixed.*	**Functions of English:** making suggestions and giving advice **Listening comprehension:** answering questions on a dialogue	autobiographical extract SB: features and assignment – people from your past WB: planning sheet

Conversation focus audio scripts   Page 122

English World map   Page 132

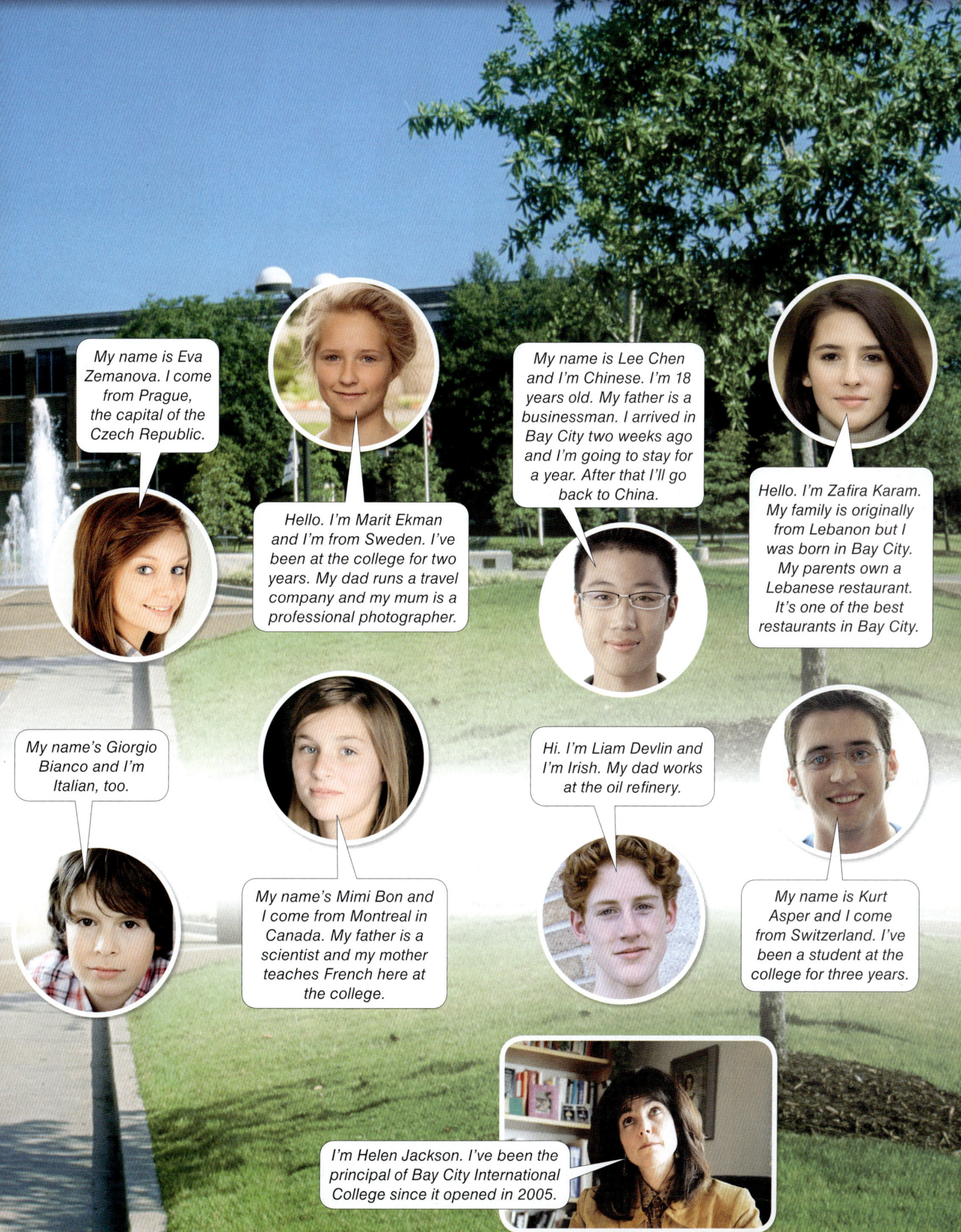

An international school

Start-up Use WB p5 for your notes.

▶ Students usually speak a variety of first languages. Most lessons are taught in one language.

▲ The school library may have books, magazines and newspapers in several languages.

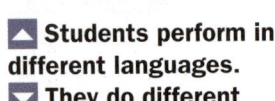
▲ Students perform in different languages.
▼ They do different sports, too.

Do you know an international school?
Do you know why some students go to an international school?
If you have studied in one, what was it like?
If you have never been in one, what do you think it would be like? Fun? Difficult? Friendly? Confusing?
Would you enjoy studying there? Why? / Why not?

Reading
- You will read three advertisements. They all appear in the school library: in a magazine, in a newspaper, on a notice board.
  Does your school have a library? What can you find there?
- They aim to persuade the reader to: buy something, give money, do something.
- The adverts are written for different readers: adults, younger teenagers, older teenagers. **Where do you see advertisements? How much time do you spend looking at advertisements each day? Which ones do you take most notice of?**

Vocabulary
- These words are in the advertisements: *livelihood   economic   absorb   biodiversity   depend   essential   affect*.
  Circle any you cannot remember or guess. Look them up.
- Find out what these phrases mean: *carbon emissions   greenhouse gas effect   carbon sink*.

Grammar
- You will study **modal verbs + passive infinitive**: *All schools have rules that **must be obeyed**.* **What school rules must you obey?**

Word focus
- Dictionary: You will look at **headwords**, which appear above the entries on each dictionary page. **What are they for?**
- Spelling: You will look at different words with **ou**. Read: *through   tough   soup   ground   double*. **How many sounds are there for *ou*?**
- Prefixes: You will look at how **prefixes** change meanings. **Underline the prefixes in *untie* and *retie*. What do they mean?**

▼ When there's a lot going on, the notice board is a good place for finding information.

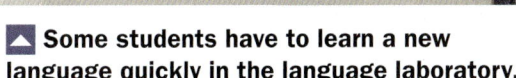

▲ Some students have to learn a new language quickly in the language laboratory.

Grammar in use

- You will hear a discussion about a festival. Festivals happen worldwide in different ways.

  What festivals do you know of? What are they like?

- People often use **question tags** in conversational English. They are useful:
  - when you expect the answer 'Yes':
    This ice cream is cold, isn't it?
  - when you expect the answer 'No':
    You're not a brain surgeon, are you?

  Make up two similar questions to ask your friend.

Listening and speaking

- You will listen to some advertisements. What product is advertised on TV most often?
- You will prepare a presentation on your views of advertising.

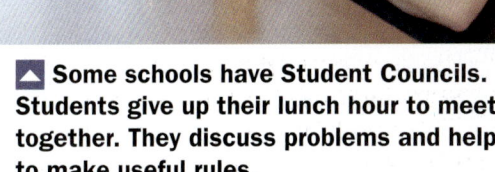

▲ Some schools have Student Councils. Students give up their lunch hour to meet together. They discuss problems and help to make useful rules.

Conversation focus

Liam and Kurt are senior students at the International School. They both do a lot of things.
1. Listen to their conversation in the school library.
2. Read the questions on Workbook page 5. Listen again and answer the questions.
3. Talk in a group about things you're doing in school or that other people are doing. Use the photos to help you and these ideas: homework tasks   projects   clubs   matches   practice sessions   competitions. Ask: *Are you coming to …? What are you doing …?* Say: *I'm going to …, I've got to …*

Writing

- You will write an advertisement. Find an advertisement that you think is very persuasive. Find one that you think is not very persuasive. Bring them to the lesson. Write where you found them in your Workbook.

Persuasion

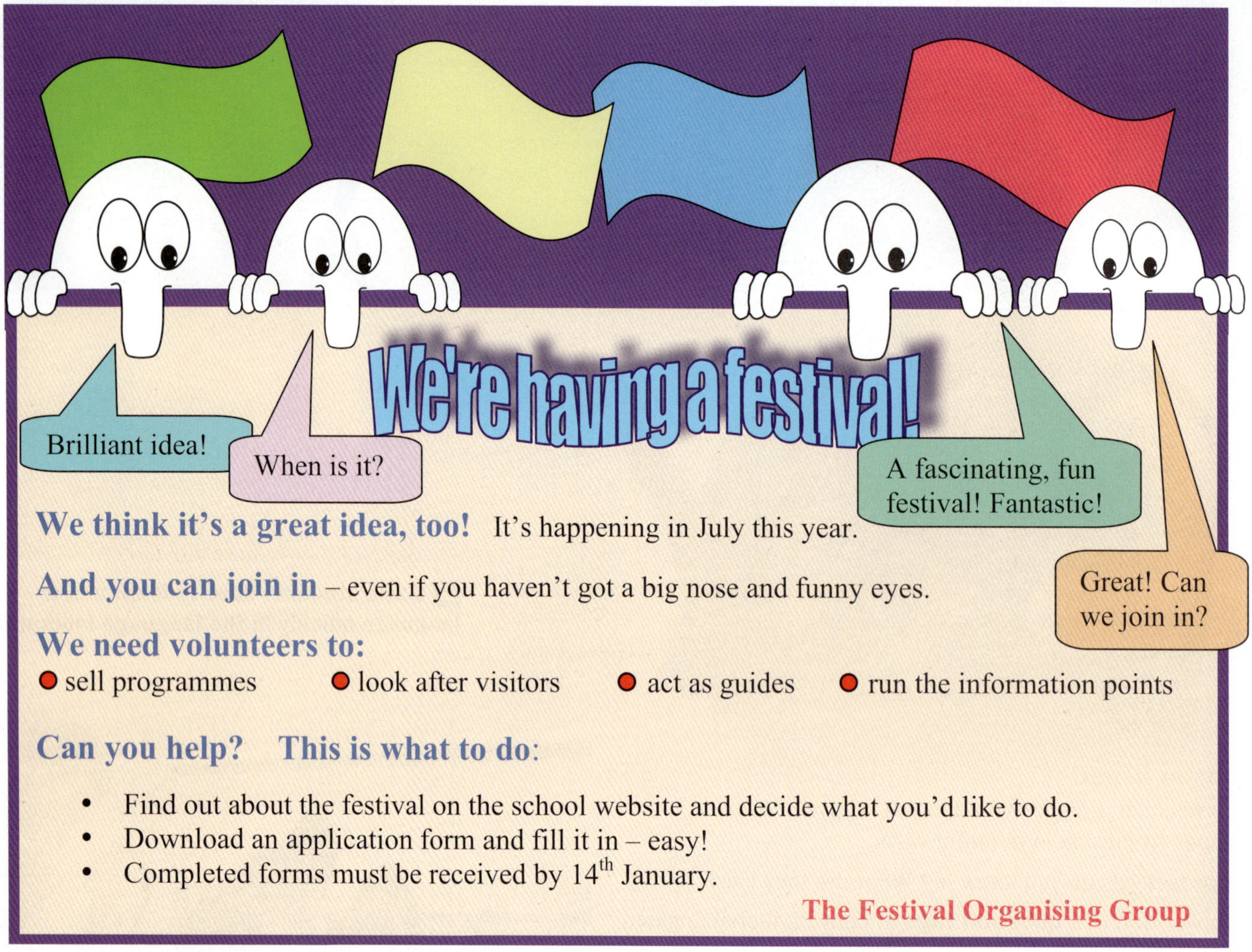

We're having a festival!

- Brilliant idea!
- When is it?
- A fascinating, fun festival! Fantastic!
- Great! Can we join in?

We think it's a great idea, too! It's happening in July this year.

And you can join in – even if you haven't got a big nose and funny eyes.

We need volunteers to:

- sell programmes
- look after visitors
- act as guides
- run the information points

Can you help? **This is what to do:**

- Find out about the festival on the school website and decide what you'd like to do.
- Download an application form and fill it in – easy!
- Completed forms must be received by 14th January.

The Festival Organising Group

You wouldn't wear boots to go running, would you?

Make the choice.

Aether

"Always my choice."
Ben Hill, Olympic® athlete

Aether trainers from the Carlton Shoe Company $200–$250. Order online at www.carltonshoes.org

A personal message from *International Forests*:
Now you really can save the planet.

You may know that carbon (CO_2) emissions are creating the greenhouse gas effect. It may surprise you to know that deforestation affects the planet more than the carbon emissions from every plane, car, truck, ship and train on the planet combined. Forests are carbon sinks. They absorb carbon and help to control the global climate, **but 80% of the world's forests have *already* been damaged or destroyed.** Each year more than 13 million hectares of forests disappear, an area roughly as big as England. To put it another way, a forest area the size of 35 football pitches is lost every minute.

If we want to limit emissions and survive climate change, the destruction has to stop.

Without healthy, thriving forests, planet Earth cannot sustain life. They are home to 80% of all terrestrial biodiversity. Tropical forests should be seen as one of the greatest storehouses of nature's diversity on Earth: of all of the world's land species, around two thirds live in forests. Many of these rare creatures – orang-utans, tigers, jaguars, forest elephants and rhinos – are increasingly threatened by extinction.

If we want to keep these animals and others, the destruction has to stop.

Forests are essential to civilisations and crucial for economic development. They offer access to water, agricultural productivity, energy, soil conservation and flood control. Over 1.6 billion people worldwide – that's nearly a quarter of the current world population – depend on forest resources for their livelihoods and many rely on forests for food, shelter and water.

"Forests affect the lives of all our people. Yet while people are dependent on forests, our forests are also dependent on people." (The Environment Minister of the Philippines speaking at the United Nations Forum on Forests, 9th session, 2011)

If we want to help people live in their forest communities, the destruction has to stop.

2011 was declared by the United Nations as the International Year of the Forest.
Let's go forward from there. *International Forests* works to preserve existing forests throughout the world and plant new ones. Together we can work for the future of our planet.

Donate now to *International Forests'* worldwide projects and stop the destruction.

You can donate online at www.international.forest.org or send cheques to:
International Forests, 740 City Road, London N22 6BW

Reading comprehension

1 **Discuss these questions.**
1 When is the festival taking place?
2 What can you do as a festival volunteer?
3 Which company makes Aether trainers?
4 What is special about Ben Hill?
5 Which causes more damage: deforestation or all the traffic and transport in the world added together?
6 What do forests offer that help civilisations to develop?
7 How much of the current world population depends on forest resources for their livelihoods?
8 Who declared 2011 to be the International Year of the Forest?

2 Read these words. Underline the compound nouns.

combine   biodiversity   greenhouse   storehouse   conserve

3 Match the words from Activity 2 to the correct definition.
1 .... the variety of plants and animals
2 .... to keep safe and in good condition
3 .... to put together
4 .... a building where things are kept for future use
5 .... a building made mostly of glass in which plants are grown

4 **Discuss these questions about advertising.**
1 Which action do you think is the most difficult to persuade people to do? Why?
  a to volunteer
  b to buy
  c to give
2 Which of these purposes do you think is the easiest to achieve?
  a encouraging school students to volunteer to help with the festival
  b getting people to spend money on new trainers
  c convincing people to give money to help protect the world's forests
3 Is the inclusion of pictures or photos important in an advert? Why? What kind of photos and illustrations do you think are most effective?

5 **Discuss your answers to these questions.**
1 Is volunteering a good thing to do? Why? / Why not?
2 The second advertisement includes an Olympic® athlete. Do you admire people who can do things very well? Why? / Why not?
3 Why do some people want to save the planet?
4 Do you think their concerns are important? Why? / Why not?
5 How do you think trees help to conserve the soil in a forest?
6 What extra danger do you think deforestation causes when there is a flood?

6 **What do you think?**
- Which advert do you think is the most eye-catching? What do you think is especially eye-catching about it?
- Which advertisement do you find most persuasive? Why?
- If you were asked to create a new advertisement for one of the purposes listed in Activity 4, which one would you choose and why?

Grammar

1 Read.

According to the charity *International Forests*, 13 million hectares of forests are lost each year. Why is this? There are many reasons. Trees **may be cut down** to provide wood for buildings or furniture. Forests **might be cleared** so that the land can be used for farming, especially raising cattle, and vast areas of forest are destroyed by large companies wanting to extract minerals or oil from the land.

Because forests absorb carbon, they help to control the world's climate. They **should be seen** as a vital weapon in the fight against global warming, one of the biggest problems of modern times.

Can the planet **be saved**? Yes, it can but steps **must be taken** immediately to stop the destruction of our forests. Please help now. The fate of our planet cannot be left to chance. Donations to this excellent charity **can be made** online at www.international.forest.org.

2 Answer these questions.
1. What area of forests is destroyed each year?
2. Why might trees be cut down? Find three reasons.
3. Why should forests be seen 'as a vital weapon in the fight against global warming'?
4. Can our planet be saved?
5. What must happen immediately?
6. How can donations be made?

3 Make these sentences passive.
1. People could use the wood to make furniture.
   The wood could be used to make furniture.
2. People might sell the land.
3. People should not cut down the trees.
4. We must take global warming seriously.
5. People ought to make donations to the charity.
6. Can we leave the fate of our planet to chance?

4 Make these sentences passive. Use *by* + phrase.
1. One or two people can't solve the problem.
   The problem can't be solved by one or two people.
2. All of us must take steps to help.
3. An oil company might buy the land.
4. Stronger laws ought to protect the forests.
5. Governments worldwide should recognise the problem.
6. Could stronger action save the forests?

5 Talk about it.
1. In your opinion, which natural habitats ought to be protected?
2. Which rare creatures are threatened with extinction? What must be done to save them?
3. Think of the natural places and creatures in your country. What should be done to look after them?
4. Think about your town or city. What could be done to improve it?

Modal verbs + passive infinitive

Formation: modal verb + *be* + past participle

Steps **must be taken** immediately.

Forests **might be cleared** to create land for farming.

Can the planet **be saved**?

The fate of our planet **should not be left** to chance.

We use the passive:
- when we do not know who does the action.
- when we do not care who does the action.
- when we know who does the action but we do not want to say.

Donations **ought to be made** at once.

We also use the passive when the person or thing that does the action is important or significant.

The land **could be bought by a powerful oil company**.

Make up sentences of your own using the passive form of *should, ought to, can, might, must*.

Word focus

A Dictionary work Headwords

A headword is the word in bold at the top of each page of a dictionary.
The word above the first column is the first word on the page. → **advantage**   **advice** ← The word above the second column is the last word on the page.
These words act as a guide to help you find the word you are looking for, e.g. adventure:
All three words – advantage / advice / adventure – begin with the letters adv.
Look at the fourth letter in each word: advantage / advice / adventure.
The word adventure will come after the word advantage and before the word advice.

1 Look at the second letter of each word.
Headwords: **emissions**   **every**
Will the word earth come before or after emissions? Before or after every?

2 Look at the third letter of each word.
Headwords: **football**   **fossil**
Will the word forest come before or after football? Before or after fossil?

3 Look at the fourth letter of each word.
Headwords: **threatened**   **thriving**
Will the word throughout come before or after threatened? Before or after thriving?

B Spelling Words with *ou*

1 Write the headings:
<u>ou</u> saying /ʌ/   <u>ou</u> saying /uː/
Sort the words under the correct heading.

rough   group   trouble   through
enough   wound   soup
country   youth   southern

2 Does this word family have an /ʌ/ sound or an /uː/ sound?

courage / discourage / encourage

Look up each word in a dictionary and use them in sentences of your own.

3 The letters *ou* can also make the sound /aʊ/. Write the words for these clues.

1 .... something you live in
2 .... talk loudly
3 .... opposite of *north*
4 .... bigger than a hill
5 .... opposite of *inside*

C Word groups Festival and forest

1 Write the headings:
<u>festival</u>   <u>forest</u>

Sort the words under the correct headings.

celebration   trees   soil   carnival
gala   hectares   jamboree
carbon   fête

2 Add two more words to the forest group and put the words into alphabetical order.

3 Write the names of two festivals in your country.

D Prefixes *de- / dis- / af- / re- / in-*

1 Find these words in the advertisements and make sure you understand the meanings.

deforestation   **dis**appear
population   **de**pendent

2 Explain the difference between:

deforestation   and   **af**forestation
disappear   and   **re**appear
population   and   **de**population
dependent   and   **in**dependent

Grammar in use

1 🎧 **Listen and read.**

Festival committee meeting – library Tuesday – 1pm sharp

Todd: Hi, everyone. Let's get started, **shall we**? We've got loads to do.
Lucie: There are more than four of us on the committee, **aren't there**? Where is everyone?
Ramon: No idea. Perhaps they've got held up.
Todd: Let's talk about what we'd like to see at the festival.
Tasha: Well, we definitely need lots of music, **don't we**?
Ramon: Classical or pop?
Tasha: Oh, both! Jazz, as well. Something for everyone.
Lucie: And dancing. We must have dancing, **mustn't we**?
Todd: What sort of dancing? Ballet? Not everyone likes ballet, **do they**?
Tasha: What about art? Could we have an art exhibition, do you think?
Ramon: Can I say something, please?
Todd: Sure. Go ahead.
Ramon: Well, we shouldn't forget about children, **should we**?
Todd: Absolutely not. What have you got in mind?
Ramon: Circus skills! You know ... tight-rope walking, juggling, walking on stilts ...
Tasha: Brilliant! Kids would love that, **wouldn't they**?
Rudi: Hi, guys! I'm late, **aren't I**? Sorry!
Lucie: Hey, Rudi! Come in! Better late than never!

2 Cover the dialogue and read the statements. Write *True* or *False*. Correct the false statements.

1. The students are discussing the festival programme.
2. Tasha would prefer to have jazz rather than classical music.
3. Todd says that everyone likes ballet.
4. The festival will be for adults only.

3 Add question tags to these statements.

1. He doesn't like swimming.
   He doesn't like swimming, does he?
2. She won't tell anyone.
3. You haven't been listening.
4. They shouldn't shout.
5. It's a beautiful day.
   It's a beautiful day, isn't it?
6. Lucie enjoys dancing.
7. Ramon suggested circus skills.
8. Children would enjoy juggling.

4 Add question tags to these statements.

1. Everyone enjoys music.
   Everyone enjoys music, don't they?
2. Anyone can dance.
3. Somebody forgot to lock the door.
4. Nobody lives here.
5. Not everyone likes jazz.
6. Everyone should help with the festival.

We use **question tags** in conversation when:
- we expect the listener to agree with a statement.
- we are unsure if the listener will agree with a statement.

1. When the sentence is negative, the question tag is affirmative.
   The shops **aren't** open, **are they**?
2. When the sentence is affirmative, the question tag is negative.
   The lady **is selling** honey, **isn't she**?
3. We use auxiliary verbs in question tags: *is, are, do, does, have, has, had, was, were, did, will, would*.
   They **went** to Spain, **didn't they**?
4. We use modal verbs in question tags: *must, should, ought, may, might, can, could*.
   She **ought to** practise, **oughtn't she**?
5. With *everybody / everyone, somebody / someone, anybody / anyone* and *nobody / no one* the verb is singular but the question tag is plural.
   Everyone **likes** ice cream, **don't they**?
   Nobody **is** laughing, **are they**?
6. Notice this exception: *I'm right, **aren't I**?*

Find examples of 1, 2, 3, 4 and 5 in the dialogue.

Grammar in use: question tags

Listening and speaking

Listening comprehension

1 Look at the pictures and write the type of product under each one.

football magazine   toothpaste   campsite   fruit juice   chewing gum

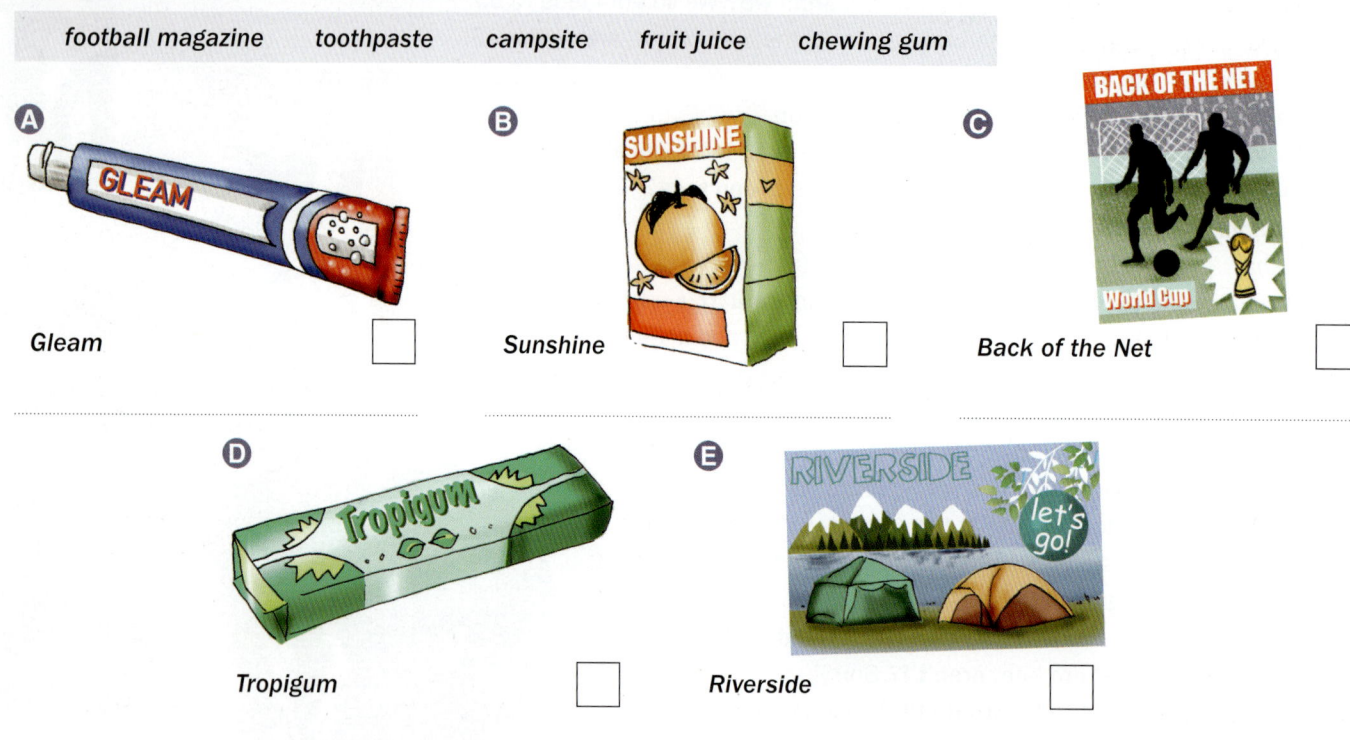

A Gleam
B Sunshine
C Back of the Net
D Tropigum
E Riverside

2 🎧 1.05 Listen and match the advertisements 1–5 to the products in Activity 1.

3 Read and choose the best answer. 🎧 1.06 Listen again. Were you right?

1 *Sunshine* is healthy because it …
   a is tasty.
   b has lots of sugar and vitamins.
   c has lots of vitamins and not much sugar.
2 At *Riverside* there are … water sports available.
   a no
   b some
   c many
3 Brushing your teeth with *Gleam* will give you …
   a a sparkling smile.
   b shiny teeth and healthy gums.
   c harmful bacteria.
4 *Tropigum* comes in … fruit flavours.
   a four
   b five
   c six
5 One *Back of the Net* reader will win … trip to a football match.
   a a free
   b a cheap
   c an expensive

4 Talk about it.

Would you buy any of the five products above? Why? / Why not?

Individual speaking

You are going to talk about advertisements.
Preparation in groups:

1 List all the places where you see or hear advertisements. How many can you think of?
2 What was the last advertisement you saw or heard? What was it for? Where was it?
3 Do you like or dislike advertising? Is there too much, too little or just the right amount?
4 Think of an advertisement which you like. What is it for? Why do you like it?
5 Think of an advertisement which you don't like. What is it for? Why don't you like it?

Now tell the rest of the class about your group discussion. **WB p11**

Writing features

Persuasive writing

Advertisements are a form of **persuasive writing**. They are written for a particular purpose and a particular audience.

Checklist
Look again at the three advertisements on pages 8 and 9.

▶ **Purpose** Discuss the *purpose* of each one. What is each one trying to persuade you to do? Which one do you think is most successful?

▶ **Audience** Discuss the *audience* each advertisement is aimed at. Which one do you think is the most successful in terms of target audience?

▶ **Beginning** Advertisements need to be noticed. How they *begin* is important.

Which one begins with a question? Why does it do this?
Which one begins with alliteration? Why does it do this?

▶ **Language** Advertisers choose language carefully. They want the advertisement to be persuasive. In the first advert, the speech bubbles don't just say 'OK'. They say 'Brilliant', 'Fantastic', 'Great!'.

Look at adverts two and three. Find examples of *persuasive language*.

▶ **Repetition** One of the adverts repeats a five-word phrase. Which one? Why does it do this?

▶ **Information** Information in advertisements can include dates, addresses, prices and statistics.

Find an example of each one in the advertisements. Discuss why they are an important part of each advertisement.

▶ **Quotes** Advertisers often use *quotes* from famous people to make an advertisement more appealing to the target audience.

Find two examples of quotes and who is quoted in the advertisements. Discuss why you think quotes from these particular people have been used.

▶ **Layout / Appearance** Advertisers spend a lot of time getting the right 'look' for their advertisement. If it doesn't appeal to the target audience, it won't be successful.

Think about the target audience for each advert and discuss the use of text / colour / illustration / font size / bold / italics. Does each advertisement attract its target audience?

Writing assignment
You have read and discussed three adverts with very different purposes and audiences. You are now going to create your own advertisement to persuade teenagers to buy a new magazine. Your magazine can be about fashion, music or sport.

Go to p12 in your Workbook for help with your planning.

Writing features: persuasive writing 15

Music

Start-up Use WB p15 for your notes.

▼ Early Western music was played by small groups of musicians for a small audience. It was usually played in a small private room and became known as chamber music.

Early chamber music group

▶ Western classical music dates from about the 18th century. Composers from countries all over Europe wrote orchestral pieces for many instruments, which were performed to larger audiences.

orchestra

soloist

▲ Orchestras got even larger, with four sections: brass, strings, woodwind and percussion. Some classical pieces feature one instrument for a soloist who plays alongside the full orchestra.

In the phrase *pop music*, what does *pop* mean?
How many of the kinds of music on this page do you know?
Do you play an instrument? If so, which one? If not, would you like to? Which one?
Have you heard music performed live? What kind of music was it?
Which do you listen to most: recorded music or live music? Why?

Reading

- You will read an email. The writer is a supporter of classical music. In the email he discusses the qualities of classical music. He says why pop music is not so good. Do you think many young people share his view? Why? / Why not?
- When you discuss different views in writing, it is called discursive writing. An email or an essay can be discursive. Think of two other forms of writing that could be discursive.

Vocabulary

- These words are in the email: *conduct* (v) *genre* *emphasise* *schedule* (n) *unreliable* *enthusiastic.* Circle any you cannot remember or guess. Look them up.
- Find out what these phrasal verbs mean: *catch on* *drop out.*

Grammar

- You will learn more about **reported questions**. You already know how to report questions in the present tense. Report this question: *"Does the next train go to London?" asked Anna.*

Word focus

- Dictionary: You will look at **words with two or more meanings** that are the same part of speech. Find two meanings for these nouns: *ruler club band.*
- Spelling: You will look at the different spellings for the /uː/ sound. Think of words of your own for these spelling patterns making a /uː/ sound: *u_e, oo, ew, ou, ue.*
- Word groups: You will look at adjectives and the prefix ***inter-***. Think of a word that uses the prefix ***inter-*** and write what the word means.

2

jazz band

▼ Now, the biggest live audiences are at pop festivals: 100,000 and more watching one band.

pop band

▲ During the 20th century, when sound recording was invented, many different kinds of music became popular.

swing band

▲▼ All different kinds of music is heard all over the world and listeners can choose any music they like of any type.

folk band

traditional music group

Grammar in use
- You will hear a discussion about the music programme for the festival.
- You will study **transitive and intransitive phrasal verbs**. What does a transitive verb have that an intransitive verb does not have?

Listening and speaking
- You will study and practise expressions for asking for and giving opinions. Think of three topics that you have strong opinions about.
- You will discuss opinions on various topics of your choice in a group.
- You will listen to a conversation about the festival music programme in which strong opinions are put forward. Do you have strong opinions about different kinds of music that you like or hate? What are they?

Conversation focus 🎧 1.07
Gustav helps to organise the school orchestra. Florence and Giorgio play in the orchestra.
1. Listen to their conversation in the music department.
2. Read the questions on Workbook page 15. Listen again and answer the questions.
3. Talk in a group about the kind of music you like. Use the photos to help you, as well as any of your own ideas. Ask: *Do you like …? Have you ever heard …?* Say: *I love …, I'd really like to see …, I prefer …*

Writing
- You will write a discursive essay. You will be asked to work out what your **attitude** is to a particular question. What does *attitude* mean?
- You have heard part of the first meeting of the festival committee at the International School. Do you think they are going to organise the festival well? Why? / Why not?

17

Classical is best!

From   Gustav Hindman
To   Festival committee
Subject Music programme

Dear festival committee,

The kind of music that we include in our festival is very important and it is absolutely essential that we get it right. Obviously, the music programme must include a wide variety of events that will appeal to many different kinds of people but, at the same time, I feel that the festival should not attract people who do not really know anything about music. I know some people will argue in favour of including pop music but classical music is far more appropriate. We have the school's reputation for excellence to consider and we should not put this at risk.

The first point is that classical music is superior to any other type of music. It is called classical for a reason: it stands the test of time and people have been playing it, listening to it and appreciating it for centuries. They know it is the best.

Next, we want to attract a broad audience. With the classical genre, that is no problem at all. There is such a wide variety of music types, composers, instruments and orchestras within the classical repertoire that we could run a classical programme for years and not repeat ourselves. With a range from early music quartets to 70-piece orchestras and everything in between, frankly, we will be spoiled for choice.

Having attracted people to the festival, we want them to come to more than one kind of event. The audience for classical music is an educated group of people who will understand and appreciate other art forms. They will be loyal and enthusiastic supporters of other festival events, such as ballet and art exhibitions.

The field of classical music contains outstandingly talented musicians. It must be clear to everyone that this is what we need in order to establish a good musical reputation for the festival. I am in a unique position to help here. My uncle conducts a small London-based chamber orchestra. I asked him if he would be able to bring his orchestra to our festival and he said he would. This is very exciting. The orchestra is well-known internationally and has had some exceptionally good reviews recently. I'm attaching some photos taken at the Berlin festival. I've got some recordings you can listen to, as well.

Finally, it is important to point out that a classical repertoire is essential for all school students as part of their general education and especially in helping them to develop a truly discerning taste in music. More than 70% of students in this school play an orchestral instrument and they will benefit enormously from seeing professional orchestras perform live.

Some people will present pop music as being a desirable part of the programme because lots of people enjoy it. It is true. Lots of people do enjoy it. A tune catches on and you hear it on the radio, on TV, on the internet and even in the supermarket. You hear it everywhere, then suddenly, it's gone. It's only popular for a short time. Pop music has no staying power and justifiably so. Most of it is not worth listening to more than a few times.

People say that there are lots of great pop performers. There probably are but that's all they are: great performers. The point is that the music has little merit. It all sounds the same. It is basically guitars and drums and not much else. I heard a pop star being interviewed the other day. The reporter asked him how he wrote his music. He said that he couldn't even read music and did it all by ear. What will this type of performer add to the standard of the festival?

The point will be made that pop music will attract a larger, younger audience. It's true. The *City Pop! festival* attracted an average of 4,000 people to most events. I asked the head teacher if we had a space big enough for such a large audience and she said that we did not.

Some people will bring up the idea that pop music is more fun but this is not an advantage. A young and inexperienced audience will get over-excited and may start to behave badly. I asked the school caretaker if he had ever had trouble with pop concerts and he said he had but, fortunately, not at this school. However, an over-excited audience is definitely something we want to avoid.

Somebody might try to make the case that pop celebrities will give the school publicity. Again, this may be true but we have to remind ourselves that things can go wrong. Celebrities often show off and look terrible. They are notoriously unreliable, cannot keep to a schedule and may drop out at the last moment. There's every chance that the school's reputation could suffer.

I conclude by emphasising the superiority of classical music and the dependability of classical musicians and the classical music audience. With this choice, the school's reputation and the events are guaranteed. In contrast, pop stars and their fans have little musical education or expertise, and the behaviour of both the performers and their audience is potentially a complete disaster. You wouldn't want to risk the school's reputation, would you? I hope you will think over my point of view and feel able to embrace a purely classical programme.

Best wishes,

Gustav

Assistant conductor, School Orchestra

Reading comprehension

1 **Discuss these questions.**
1. What kind of music does Gustav think is appropriate for the festival?
2. How long have people been listening to classical music?
3. What other events does he think the classical music audience will enjoy?
4. What percentage of students at the school play an orchestral instrument?
5. What places does Gustav say you can hear pop music?
6. What instruments does Gustav say that pop musicians use?
7. Which staff at the school did Gustav talk to about pop concerts?
8. What does Gustav want the festival committee to do?

2 **Match these phrases from the text to the correct definition.**

| the test of time | spoiled for choice | staying power | make the case |
| in contrast | at risk | in favour of | by ear |

1. .... the ability and strength to go on for a long time
2. .... in danger
3. .... having a large amount of something available
4. .... how good something continues to be over a long period
5. .... in support of
6. .... using natural ability to recognise sounds accurately
7. .... present the argument
8. .... completely opposite to

Stuck? Remember to think about the words you already know within each phrase.

3 **Discuss these questions about the discursive style of Gustav's email.**
1. How does he divide up the email?
2. Which paragraphs mention both classical music *and* pop music?
3. How many paragraphs does he write that explain the good things about classical music?
4. How many paragraph does he write that explain the bad things about pop music?
5. What is the very last point that he makes?

4 **Discuss your answers to these questions.**
1. Do you agree with anything Gustav says about classical music? List the points you agree with. Say why you disagree with any others.
2. Do you agree with anything Gustav says about pop music? List the points you agree with. Say why you disagree with any others.
3. Do you think most people like a) only classical, b) only pop or c) a mixture of both? What reasons do you have to support your answer?

5 **What do you think?**
- If you were on the committee, what would you say about Gustav's email?
- Do you have a strong preference for either classical or pop music? Why? / Why not?
- Imagine you have a completely free choice. List three different pieces of music you would include in the festival programme. Explain why you chose them.

Grammar

1 Read.

Gustav Hindman adores classical music but hates pop music. He did not want pop music to be included in the arts festival and he sent an email about this to the festival committee. He **wanted to know why they were thinking** of including pop music in the programme and he **asked whether they had considered** all the problems that a pop concert could cause for the school.
He **wanted to know where a large pop concert could be held**. He said that there certainly wasn't enough space at the school. He **asked the committee if they knew that young pop fans were sometimes badly behaved** and he **wondered if the school's reputation would be damaged**. He **asked the committee if they would reconsider** their plans and invite only classical musicians to the festival.

2 Cover the text and read the statements. Write *True* or *False*. Correct the false statements.

1. Gustav is a classical music fan. ....
2. He thinks pop music should be included in the festival. ....
3. He sent a text to the committee. ....
4. He thought a pop concert would not attract many people. ....
5. He thought a pop concert would be bad for the school's reputation. ....

3 Look at these direct questions. Match them to the reported questions in the text. Say how the underlined verbs change.

1. "<u>Do</u> you <u>know</u> that pop fans are sometimes badly behaved?"
2. "<u>Have</u> you <u>considered</u> all the problems that a pop concert could cause?"
3. "Why <u>are</u> you <u>thinking</u> of including pop music in the programme?"
4. "<u>Will</u> you <u>reconsider</u> your plans?"
5. "Where <u>can</u> a large pop concert <u>be held</u>?"
6. "<u>Will</u> the school's reputation <u>be damaged</u>?"

4 Report the following questions.

1. "Do you like pop music, Lucie?"
   Gustav asked Lucie ...
2. "Has anyone seen Rudi?"
   Todd wanted to know ...
3. "What are you discussing?"
   Rudi asked the committee ...
4. "Why did Gustav send an email?" Tasha asked ...
5. "Has Gustav been complaining?" Lucie asked ...
6. "What was the orchestra practising?"
   Ramon wondered ...
7. "When will the festival take place?"
   Some students asked ...
8. "Can the committee answer my questions?"
   Gustav asked ...

Reported questions

We report questions using *if / whether* or question words (*why, how,* etc.).
When the reporting verb is in the **present** tense, the tense of the verb in the question does not change.
*"When **is** the orchestra arriving?"* →
*Jen wants to know when the orchestra **is** arriving.*
When the reporting verb is in the **past** tense, the tense of the verb in the question usually changes.
**present simple / continuous / perfect →
past simple / continuous / perfect**
*"Where **is** the orchestra?"* →
*He wanted to know where the orchestra **was**.*
*"**Have** the musicians **arrived**?"* →
*He asked if the musicians **had arrived**.*
**past simple / continuous →
past perfect simple / continuous**
*"**Did** you **buy** anything?"* →
*She asked me whether I **had bought** anything.*
*"What **has** Tom **been doing**?"* →
*He asked what Tom **had been doing**.*
will / can → would / could
*"When **will** the concert start?"* →
*They asked when the concert **would** start.*
*"**Can** I buy a ticket?"* →
*She wondered whether she **could** buy a ticket.*
There are no question marks in reported questions.
Be very careful with word order!

Word focus

A Dictionary work Words with two or more meanings (1)

Some words have **more than one meaning**, even though they are the **same part of speech**.

festival	/'festɪv(ə)l/	noun [C]	1 a series of performances of films, plays, music or dancing that is usually organised in the same place at the same time each year
			2 a day or period when there is a public holiday, often to celebrate a religious event

1 Choose the correct definition for each word as it is used in the email.

1. instrument
   a. a tool that is used in science, medicine or technology
   b. piano, guitar, flute, etc.
2. broad
   a. wide
   b. including many different things or people
3. audience
   a. the people who watch or listen to a performance
   b. a formal meeting with a very important person
4. disaster
   a. something very bad that happens and causes a lot of damage or kills a lot of people
   b. a very bad or annoying situation, or a complete failure

2 Write a sentence of your own for each of the words above.
Use the definition of each word that is not used in the email.

B Spelling Words with the /uː/ sound

Words with the /uː/ sound can be spelled:
  u_e: **tune**   oo: **school**   ue: **true**
  ew: **few**   ou: gr**ou**p

1 Write the **u_e** words for these definitions.
  1 a plan of activities and events,
     and when they will happen   s _ _ _ _ _ _ _
  2 to make someone or something part
     of a group, collection or set   i _ _ _ _ _ _ _
  3 a musical instrument   f _ _ _ _
  4 another word for *scent*   p _ _ _ _ _ _

2 Write the irregular past tense of these verbs.
  blow   draw   grow   throw

3 Complete these words with **ou, ue** or **oo**.
  1 ch _ _ se   2 y _ _ th
  3 arg _ _   4 thr _ _ gh
  5 f _ _ lish   6 gl _ _

C Word groups Positive and negative adjectives

1 Write the headings:
  positive   **negative**

Sort the adjectives under the correct heading as they are used in the email.

  **superior   terrible   educated
  unreliable   over-excited   discerning**

2 Write a group of at least five words to do with music that you can find in the email.

D Prefixes *inter-*

*The orchestra is well-known **inter**nationally.*
• The prefix *inter-* means 'among' or 'between'.

1 What do these *inter-* words mean? Use your dictionary to help you.

  **interactive   intercept   interject
  interlude   intermediary   interview**

2 Use two of the *inter-* words in sentences of your own.

Grammar in use

Festival committee meeting – common room – today – 12pm Don't be late!

1 🔊 1.09 **Listen and read.**

Todd: OK ... I think we've all **looked through** Gustav's email.
Tasha: I don't even know why we're discussing it. It's perfectly ridiculous!
Lucie: **Calm down**, Tasha! Gustav **is putting forward** some serious points.
Rudi: Well, it's true that we can't **put on** a pop concert for 4,000 people.
Ramon: But 1,000 spectators would be perfectly OK.
Tasha: Can I **point out** that not all pop fans are badly behaved?
Ramon: And the pop group we're having is not going to **drop out**!
Lucie: I **heard from** them this morning. They'**re looking forward to** it.
Rudi: **Hang on** a minute! Who is this band?
Lucie: *The River Boys*. We **settled on** them last week.
Tasha: You didn't **show up** for that meeting on time, Rudi ...
Todd: So are we all agreed? We want to include all kinds of music?
Ramon: Absolutely! We want pop, jazz, folk and classical.
Rudi: Shall we **find out** if Gustav's uncle can bring his chamber orchestra?
Lucie: Yes, definitely. They sound fantastic.
Todd: OK. I'll contact Gustav today and see what we can **sort out**.

2 Answer these questions.
1 What does the committee think of Gustav's email?
2 How big a pop concert can they put on?
3 Do *The River Boys* sound like an irresponsible band? Why? / Why not?
4 What sort of music do they want at the festival?

3 Match the verbs in the box to the underlined phrasal verbs below.

| decide on | said, stated | left unexpectedly |
| organise, arrange | wait | appear, arrive |

1 Please, <u>hang on</u> a second! You're walking too fast!
2 After a lot of discussion we finally <u>settled on</u> Spain for our holiday.
3 We need to <u>sort out</u> our flights to Madrid.
4 John wasn't enjoying acting in the school play, so he <u>dropped out</u>.
5 The match was abandoned because the referee didn't <u>show up</u>.
6 Gustav <u>pointed out</u> that his uncle was a conductor.

4 Complete these sentences with the phrasal verbs in the box. Make sure you use the correct form of the verb.

| look through | calm down | put on |
| look forward to | find out | catch on |

1 He's a fascinating writer. I'd like to .... more about him.
2 Her fashion designs were interesting but they never ....
3 Why are you all shouting? .... at once!
4 Would you mind .... my essay and checking the spelling?
5 The drama club is going to .... a play by Shakespeare.
6 The students .... really .... their trip to London.

Phrasal verbs
Some phrasal verbs are **transitive**. They always have an **object**.
    I'll **think over** your suggestions.
Other phrasal verbs are **intransitive**. They do not have an **object**.
    He never discovered how the accident **came about**.
Some phrasal verbs can be both transitive and intransitive.
    The doors of the bus opened and we **got on**.
    We **got on** the bus.

Find examples of transitive and intransitive phrasal verbs in the dialogue in Activity 1.

Grammar in use: transitive and intransitive phrasal verbs

Listening and speaking

Functions of English: asking for and giving opinions

1 Look at these useful expressions.

> I think ...   I believe ...   I feel ...   In my opinion, ...   To my mind, ...
> As far as I'm concerned, ...   If you ask me, ...   To be honest, ...

Give your opinion. Answer these questions using the expressions above.
1 What do you think of classical music?
2 What do you think of pop music?
3 What do you think of exams?
4 What do you think of zoos?

2 Look at these useful expressions for expressing strong opinions.

> I'm sure that ...   I strongly believe that ...   I definitely think that ...
> I'm absolutely convinced that ...   I have no doubt whatsoever that ...

Give your opinion. Answer these questions using the expressions above.
1 What changes do you think should be made in your school?
2 What problems will your town face in the future? How can these problems be solved?
3 What do you think you will be doing in ten years' time?

3 Group conversation

How can you ask for opinions?

> What do you think of ...?   How do you feel about ...?   What's your view on ...?
> What's your opinion of / about ...?   Do you have any thoughts about ...?

What can you say if you don't have an opinion?

> That's an interesting question.   I haven't really thought about this before.
> I'm not entirely sure.   Could I have a moment to think about this?

Write three questions asking for opinions on any topic.
Work in small groups. Ask and answer. Find out each other's opinions.
Use expressions from all the boxes.

Listening comprehension

1 🎧 Listen to a conversation and answer these questions.
1 Who is Miss Jackson?
2 Why is this meeting taking place?
3 What is the outcome of the conversation?

2 🎧 Listen again and answer these questions.
1 Where do you think this meeting is taking place?
2 Who asked for the meeting? Why?
3 According to Gustav, how did the committee deal with his email?
4 Does Todd agree with him?
5 What is Gustav's main concern about pop fans?
6 What does Miss Jackson think about pop music? How do you know?
7 What is Miss Jackson's opinion of the festival committee?
8 Does she think the festival will be a success? How do you know?

3 Who do you agree with? Give reasons.

Writing features

Discursive writing

> A **discursive essay** is one in which the writer presents facts, ideas and opinions about a given subject and arrives at a conclusion supported by reasons.

Checklist
Look again at Gustav's email on pages 18 and 19.

- **Subject**
  A discursive piece of writing has a particular *subject*.
  What is the subject of Gustav's email?

- **Purpose**
  A discursive piece of writing has a particular *purpose*.
  Discuss the purpose of the email. Why is Gustav writing to the festival committee?
  What is he hoping to persuade them to do?

- **Opening paragraph**
  The *first paragraph* of a discursive piece of writing must make it clear to the reader what is being discussed and the attitude of the writer, i.e. which side of the argument he/she is on.
  Find one sentence in the opening paragraph that clearly states:
  - the subject.
  - the writer's attitude.

- **For and against**
  In discursive writing, the writer must look at *both sides of the argument*.
  - Gustav is for classical music.

  Read paragraphs 2–6 of the email and make a list of why he wants classical music in the festival.

  - Gustav considers the arguments for including pop music but gives his reasons why the committee shouldn't include it.

  Read paragraphs 7–11 of the email and make a list of why other people will want pop music in the festival, together with the reasons why he does not think it is a good idea.
  Why does he use five paragraphs?

- **Final paragraph**
  The final paragraph of discursive writing summarises the points that have been made before and comes to a conclusion.
  What points does Gustav repeat that support including classical music in the festival?
  What points does Gustav repeat that are against including pop music in the festival?

- **Persuasive language**
  Obviously, Gustav wants the committee to agree with his arguments. He uses very *positive* persuasive language when he is arguing for classical music, e.g. *superior, stands the test of time*.
  Find other examples of positive persuasive language in the email.
  He uses *negative* persuasive language when he is discussing pop music, e.g. *no staying power, little merit*.
  Find other examples of negative persuasive language in the email.

- **Facts**
  Gustav uses *facts* to support his opinion of classical music and pop music.
  He doesn't just write *a lot of students in this school play an orchestral instrument*. What statistic does he use?
  He doesn't just write *City Pop! festival attracted a lot of people*. What statistic does he use?

Writing assignment
You have read and discussed an email in a discursive style. You are now going to write a discursive essay.
Some people think that pupils should be involved in decisions about their school and should have a say in how things are run. Other people think that pupils are too young to take part in such important decisions. What can you say for and against pupils being involved in the running of their school?

> *Go to p22 in your Workbook for help with your planning.*

Writing features: discursive writing

Study skills 1

Paragraphs

What is a paragraph?
A paragraph is a group of sentences about one main idea.
Paragraphs help the reader because they show how a piece of writing is organised.

1 How do I begin a new paragraph?

- In a **story** or **informal letter**, leave a space of about 20mm from the left hand margin each time you begin a new paragraph.

- When you are writing **non-fiction**, you can either leave a space from the left hand margin or leave a line between each paragraph.

> On her way to school Amy was very worried. She had lost the letter Mum had asked her to post and she knew it was a very important letter!
>
> When she came home from school, Amy began to search everywhere for the letter.

> Keeping animals in zoos is cruel for many reasons.
>
> Firstly, they have so little space in which to move around …
>
> Animals should find their food, not have it given to them at set times in the day …

2 When do I begin a new paragraph?

When you begin a new paragraph depends on the type of writing you are doing.

- **Story writing**
  Begin a new paragraph:
  when something new happens.
  when you introduce a new character.
  each time a character speaks.
  when the setting changes.
  when the time changes.

Activity

Write the next two paragraphs of Amy's search for the letter.
Does Amy find the letter? When? Where?
Does Mum come home? When?
Do they have a conversation?

- **Informal letter**
  Informal letters can be very like stories. You usually write about several different things. Begin a new paragraph when you write about a new subject, e.g.
  your family
  what you have been doing at home
  where you have been
  unusual news
  things you want to know

Activity

Write a letter to a friend in three short paragraphs:
1 something unusual that happened in school
2 what you did at the weekend
3 ask when your friend is coming to visit you and suggest when would be a good time

- **Information writing**
  When you write an information text, you write about different aspects of the topic. Your first paragraph introduces the topic. Begin a new paragraph for each new aspect of the topic.

Activity

Title: My Family
Write a short paragraph on each member of your family who lives in your house.

- **Explanation**
  A piece of writing that explains something needs to be written in a logical order. It explains how or why something happens. Your first paragraph says what you are explaining. Begin a new paragraph for each stage in the process.

> **Useful paragraph beginnings:**
> First ... Second ... Third ...
> Next ... After that ... Finally ...

Activity

Write an explanation of how you travel to school. Use a new paragraph for each different way you travel, e.g.
P1: walk (to the bus stop)
P2: ride (on the bus)
P3: walk (from the bus to the school)

- **Expressing a point of view**
  When you express a point of view you give your opinion with reasons.
  Order your paragraphs like this:
  introduction: clearly state the issue
  use a new paragraph for each reason
  conclusion: summarise your reasons

> **Useful paragraph beginnings:**
> I do / don't believe ...
> It is obvious that ...
> One reason ...
> Another reason ...
> In conclusion ...

Activity

Decide if you think you *should* or *shouldn't* clean and tidy your room weekly. Think of at least two reasons for your point of view.
Express your point of view in four short paragraphs:
P1: what you are expressing your point of view about
P2: your first reason
P3: your second reason
P4: conclusion

- **Balanced argument**
  Sometimes you are asked to write arguments *for* and *against* an issue with reasons.
  Order your paragraphs like this:
  introduction: clearly state the issue
  use a new paragraph for each reason *for*
  use a new paragraph for each reason *against*
  conclusion: state whether you are *for* or *against* with reasons

> **Useful paragraph beginnings:**
> People have different opinions ...
> Some people think ... while others ...
> The main reason for / against ...
> Other reasons ...
> Looking at both side of the argument I think ...

Activity

Think of one reason for and one reason against:
Students in secondary school should do two hours homework each night.
Write your balanced argument in four short paragraphs:
P1: explain the issue that people disagree about
P2: write the reason for
P3: write the reason against
P4: your conclusion

> WB p116

It's a mystery ...

Start-up Use WB p27 for your notes.

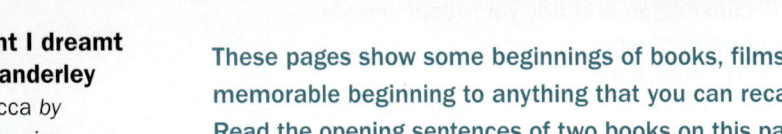
When the doorbell rings at three in the morning, it's never good news. Stormbreaker by Anthony Horowitz

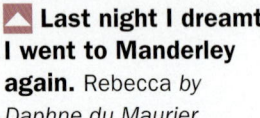
Last night I dreamt I went to Manderley again. Rebecca by Daphne du Maurier

These pages show some beginnings of books, films and events. What is the most memorable beginning to anything that you can recall?
Read the opening sentences of two books on this page. What must already have happened before each of these stories begins?
Read the opening sentences of two books on page 29. What strange facts are in them?
What kind of story beginning do you prefer? Describe it using adjectives and / or phrases.

Reading

- You will read a story with an unusual opening. The story starts in the middle of the plot when some important events have already happened. What is the usual order for a plot? The reader finds out about these events as the story continues but the opening raises a lot of questions that the reader cannot answer. Why do you think a writer might begin a story in the middle of the plot?

Vocabulary

- These words are in the story: *mile   beacon   blink   bump   distressed   ridge*. Circle any you cannot remember or guess. Look them up.
- Find out what these phrases mean: *to be sure to   What's the use?   pretty sure.*

Grammar

- You will **study participle clauses using present and past participles**. What are the present and past participles of these verbs: *lose   fall   make   suspect   drive*?

Word focus

- Dictionary: You will study **words of different classes with two or more meanings**. Think of meanings for these words as a verb and a noun: *walk   smoke   ring*.
- Spelling: You will look at the different spellings for the /eɪ/ sound. Think of words of your own for these spelling patterns: *a_e, ai, ay*.
- Prefixes: You will look at the prefix *bi-*. You know *bicycle*. What could the prefix *bi-* mean?

◀ **When Mr Bilbo Baggins of Bag End announced that he would shortly be celebrating his eleventyfirst birthday with a party of special magnificence, there was much talk and excitement in Hobbiton.** The Lord of the Rings *by JRR Tolkien*

3

Grammar in use
- You will hear a discussion about organising the festival and recruiting volunteers. **What do you think *to recruit* means? Why would the organisers want to recruit volunteers?**
- You will study **modal verbs + perfect infinitive**. **Think about the last essay you wrote. Write down three things you could have done to improve it.**

Listening and speaking
- You will listen to the festival committee making plans and deciding what each of them will be responsible for. **What does *responsible for* mean?**
- You will prepare a presentation on an event that you have helped to organise. **What are your favourite tasks when you help to organise something?**

Conversation focus 🎧 1.11
Florence and Mimi are interested in all the arts and they are looking forward to the festival.
1. Listen to their conversation when they meet by the school notice board.
2. Read the questions on Workbook page 27. Listen again and answer the questions.
3. Talk in a group about interesting or impressive openings. Discuss how you would choose to open the arts festival. Use the photos to help you, as well as any of your own ideas. Ask: *How would you open …?* Say: *My favourite film begins …, I'd open the festival with …*

Writing
- You will review the features of story writing. **The plot is a key feature. Think of two more features of story writing.**
- You will study the features of a story with an unusual opening. **Why do you think a writer might choose to create an unusual and mysterious opening to a story?**
- You will write your own unusual opening to your own story.

▼ **It was a bright, cold day in April and the clocks were striking thirteen.** 1984 *by George Orwell*

29

Z for Zachariah

A figure is staring at a spot on the horizon. Looking through a pair of binoculars, this person sees a column of smoke. Frightened by what this could mean, the person watches day by day as the column of smoke comes closer.

May 20th

I am afraid.

Someone is coming.

That is, I think someone is coming, though I am not sure, and I pray that I am wrong …

But there is smoke. For three days there has been smoke, not like the time before. That time, last year, it rose in a great cloud a long way away, and stayed in the sky for two weeks. A forest fire in the dead woods, and then it rained, and the smoke stopped. But this time it is a thin column, like a pole, not very high.

And the column has come three times, each time in the late afternoon. At night I cannot see it, and in the morning it is gone. But each afternoon it comes again, and it is nearer. At first, it was behind Claypole Ridge and I could only see the top of it, the smallest smudge. I thought it was a cloud, except that it was too grey, the wrong colour, and then I thought: there are no clouds anywhere else. I got the binoculars and saw that it was narrow and straight; it was smoke from a small fire. When we used to go in the truck, Claypole Ridge was fifteen miles, though it looks closer, and the smoke was coming from behind that.

Beyond Claypole Ridge there is Ogdentown, about ten miles further. But there is no one left alive in Ogdentown.

I know, because after the war ended, and all the telephones went dead, my father, my brother Joseph and cousin David went in the truck to find out what was happening, and the first place they went was Ogdentown. They went there early in the morning; Joseph and David were really excited, but Father looked serious.

When they came back it was dark. Mother had been worrying – they took so long – so we were glad to see the truck lights finally coming over Burden Hill, six miles away. They looked like beacons. They were the only lights anywhere, except in the house – no other cars had come down all day. We knew it was the truck because one of the lights, the left one, always blinked when it went over a bump. It came up to the house and they got out; the boys weren't excited anymore. They looked scared, and my father looked sick. Maybe he was beginning to be sick, but mainly I think he was distressed.

My mother looked at him as he climbed down.

"What did you find?"

He said, "Bodies. Just dead bodies. They're all dead."

"All?"

We went inside the house where the lamps were lit, the two boys following, not saying anything. My father sat down. "Terrible," he said, and again, "Terrible, terrible. We drove around, looking. We blew the horn. Then we went to the church and rang the bell. You can hear it five miles away. I went into a couple of houses – the Johnsons', the Peters' – they were all in there, all dead. There were dead birds all over the streets."

My brother Joseph began to cry. He was fourteen. I think I had not heard him cry for six years.

30 Reading: a story with an unusual opening

May 21st

It is coming closer. Today it was almost on top of the ridge, though not quite, because when I looked with the binoculars I could not see the flame, but still only smoke – rising very fast, not far above the fire. I know where it is: at the crossroads. Just on the other side of the ridge, the east-west highway, the Dean Town road, crosses our road. It is Route number nine, a State highway, bigger than our road, which is Country road 793. He has stopped there and is deciding whether to follow number nine or come over the ridge. I say *he* because that is what I think of, though it could be *they* or even *she*. But I think it is *he*. If he decides to follow the highway he will go away, and everything will be all right again. Why would he come back? But if he comes to the top of the ridge, he is sure to come down here, because he will see the green leaves. On the other side of the ridge, even on the other side of Burden Hill, there are no leaves; everything is dead.

There are some things I need to explain. One is why I am afraid. Another is why I am writing in this composition book, which I got from Klein's store a mile up the road. By then the last radio station, a very faint one that I could hear only at night, had stopped broadcasting. It had been dead for about three or four months. I say about, and that is one reason I got the book; because I discovered I was forgetting when things happened, and sometimes even whether things happened or not. Another reason I got it is that writing it might be like having someone to talk to, and if I read it back later it would be like someone talking to me. But the truth is I haven't written in it much after all, because there isn't much to write about.

Sometimes I would put in what the weather was like, if there was a storm or something unusual. I put in when I planted the garden because I thought that would be useful to know next year. But most of the time I didn't write, because one day was just like the day before, and sometimes I thought – what's the use of writing anyway, when nobody is ever going to read it? Then I would remind myself: some time, some years from now, you're going to read it. I was pretty sure I was the only person left in the world.

But now I have something to write about. I was wrong. I am not the only person left in the world. I am both excited and afraid.

by Robert O'Brien

Reading comprehension

1 **Discuss these questions.**
1 What does the narrator see through her binoculars?
2 At what time of day does she see it?
3 How far away is Claypole Ridge?
4 What did the narrator's father find in Ogdentown?
5 What will happen if *he* follows the highway?
6 If *he* 'comes to the top of the ridge', why will *he* 'come down' to where the narrator is?
7 What reasons does the narrator give for writing in the composition book?
8 Why hasn't the narrator written very much?

2 **Find words in the extract that mean:**
1 .... the long, narrow top of a mountain or group of mountains
2 .... a small, untidy mark
3 .... unhappy / worried
4 .... not strong or clear

3 **Find these phrases in the extract. Match the phrases in bold to the definitions in the box.**

| is certain to | travelled down the hill | in actual fact | stopped working | fine |

1 all the telephones **went dead** ....
2 no other cars had **come down** all day ....
3 everything will be **all right** again ....
4 he **is sure to** come down here ....
5 **the truth is** I haven't written in it much ....

4 **Discuss your answers to these questions.**
1 Why do you think the smoke is there in the late afternoon but not in the morning?
2 The narrator's father, brother and cousin went to Ogdentown after the telephones went dead. Why do you think:
   a 'Joseph and David were really excited'?   b 'Father looked serious'?
3 Why do you think the narrator's father 'went to the church and rang the bell' in Ogdentown?
4 How do you know that the narrator has been to 'the other side of Burden Hill'?
5 Explain in your own words why you think the narrator is 'both excited and afraid' at the end of the extract.
6 The narrator mentions that 'the war ended'. What sort of 'war' do you think has taken place? Use evidence from the extract to support your opinion.

5 **Discuss these questions about story openings.**
1 In what way is the opening to the story unusual?
2 Why do you think the writer did not begin the story by explaining all about the war and what had happened to the narrator's family?
3 Reread the extract.
   a Write brief notes on what you know about the narrator and what has happened.
   b Write a list of questions you would like to ask the narrator.

6 **What do you think?**
If you were in her position, how do you think you would feel? Think about:
- being alone for so long.
- realising that 'someone' was coming.
- how you would cope on your own.
- what you would hope for / be afraid of.

Grammar

1 Read.

Having lost all her family in a terrible war, Ann Burden found herself living alone on the family farm. She had no contact with anyone. The telephones were dead and the last radio station had stopped broadcasting long ago. **After living** alone for many months, Ann began to think that she was the only person left in the world. She started to keep a diary. She thought that **by writing** down everything that happened, she would feel less alone. It would be like having someone to talk to.

One day, **looking** through her binoculars, Ann saw a thin column of smoke. **Frightened** by what this might mean, she watched day by day as the column of smoke came closer. **Having been convinced** that she was quite alone in the world, Ann was shocked. Someone else had survived the war and, slowly but surely, that person was coming nearer.

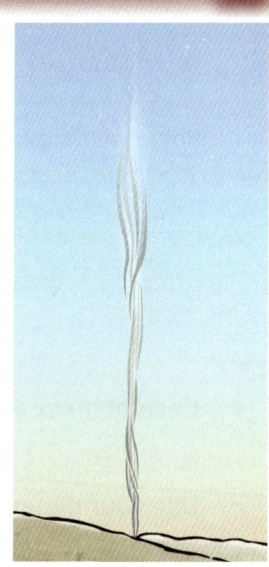

2 Answer these questions.
1. Why was Ann living alone on the farm?
2. Why did Ann think she was the last person alive in the world?
3. Why did she start to keep a diary?
4. What did the column of smoke signify?
5. Why was Ann concerned about this?

3 Find the correct endings. Write the letters.
1. Cheering wildly, ...
2. Having read about this film, ...
3. Neglected for years, ...
4. Having been chosen to be in the team, ...
5. Instead of driving to work, ...

a. the garden resembled a jungle.
b. Miss Brown decided to walk.
c. Harry was determined to play well.
d. the spectators celebrated their team's win.
e. I can't wait to see it.

4 Look at the five types of participle clause in Activity 3 above. Make sentences using similar participle clauses. Remember! Both clauses must have the same subject.
1. ..., he realised he was not alone.
2. ..., she decided to become a doctor.
3. ..., the bridge was no longer safe.
4. ..., John went to bed.
5. ..., you will soon become fluent.

Participle clauses

1. With participle clauses we use fewer words to express an idea.
When he arrived at the station, James bought a ticket.
Arriving *at the station, James bought a ticket.*

2. We use the present participle when two actions are happening at the same time.
Smiling *cheerfully, Simon greeted his guests.*

3. When one action is completed before the next starts, we can use *having* + past participle.
Having finished *his work, he went home.*

4. Passive sentences can also be expressed in fewer words by using participle clauses.
The boat was damaged by the storm and sank.
Damaged *by the storm, the boat sank.*
Or: ***Having been damaged*** *by the storm, the boat sank.*

5. Notice how prepositions (*when, while, before, after, on, instead of, without, by*) can be used in participle clauses.
Before going *to bed, he turned off the lights.*
On arriving *at the airport, we checked in.*
Without thinking*, he dived into the river.*
In all the sentences above, notice how both clauses have the same subject.

Look at the text in Activity 1. Find examples of participle clauses shown in 1–5 in the box above.

Grammar: participle clauses **33**

Word focus

A Dictionary work Words with two or more meanings (2)

Some words have **two or more meanings** because they are **different parts of speech**.

| rose¹ | /rəʊz/ | noun [C] | a flower that has a sweet smell and sharp thorns on its stem, or the bush that it grows on |
| rose² | /rəʊz/ | verb | the past tense of rise |

1 Each of these words appear in the extract. Find each one and say what part of speech it is in the extract.

   1 smoke   2 fire   3 left   4 cry   5 book   6 reason

2 Use your dictionary to find what other part of speech each word can be.

3 Choose three of the words and write sentences to show the meaning for each part of speech, e.g.
- noun = The **smoke** from the fire made us cough.
- verb = The fire was still **smoking** next morning.

B Spelling Words with the /eɪ/ sound

Words with the /eɪ/ sound can be spelled:
a_e: l**a**t**e**
ai: **ai**fraid
ay: st**ay**ed

1 Find three examples of each spelling pattern in the extract where the sound is a /eɪ/.

2 Write the a_e words for these definitions.

  1 not real   f _ _ _
  2 past tense of *make*   m _ _ _
  3 a play is performed on this   s _ _ _ _
  4 past tense of *come*   c _ _ _
  5 not early or on time   l _ _ _

3 Complete these words with *ai* or *ay*.

  1 You wear a belt around your w _ _ st.
  2 The shop had a wonderful displ _ _.
  3 The flowers sw _ _ ed in the wind.
  4 I am looking forward to my holid _ _.
  5 A train runs on a r _ _ lway line.

C Word groups Time and weather

1 Write the headings:

<u>time</u>   <u>weather</u>

Sort the words under the correct heading.

   night   morning   cloud   day   storm
        year   sky   afternoon   rain

2 Add two more words to each group and put the words into alphabetical order.

D Prefixes *bi-* / *tele-*

The narrator looked through **bi**noculars.
The prefix **bi-** means 'two'.

1 What do these *bi-* words mean? Use your dictionary to help you.

   bicentenary   bicycle   biennial
   bilateral   biped   bilingual

All the **tele**phones went dead.
The prefix **tele-** means 'at a distance'.

2 What do these *tele-* words mean? Use your dictionary to help you.

   telescope   television   telegraph   telepathy

3 Use two *bi-* words and two *tele-* words in sentences of your own.

Grammar in use

Festival meeting
Today – 1pm, library

3

1 🎧 Listen and read.

Todd: Quiet, please! This meeting **ought to have started** ten minutes ago.
Tasha: What's on the agenda, Todd?
Todd: Well, first of all tickets, programmes and posters. We need to design them.
Lucie: **Shouldn't** we **have thought** about this before? Coming up with a good design takes time, you know.
Todd: We **couldn't have discussed** it earlier. We've all been so busy.
Ramon: Who's going to print the tickets and posters and programmes?
Tasha: My uncle can do that. He has a printing firm.
Todd: Really? You **should have said** something before.
Tasha: I did! Several times!
Todd: Oh, sorry! I **must have forgotten**.
Rudi: We need to recruit lots of helpers.
Lucie: Absolutely! To sell tickets and programmes. To answer enquiries.
Ramon: And to help during the festival. To show the audience to their seats – that sort of thing.
Rudi: And to sell refreshments.
Tasha: We need some application forms for people to fill in and say what they'd like to do. I think I **might have mentioned** this before.
Todd: I can't remember but it's a good idea. Who'd like to organise that?

2 Answer these questions.

1. Did the meeting start on time?
2. What are they going to discuss?
3. How can Tasha's uncle help?
4. What will the helpers do?
5. Why are application forms a good idea?

3 Complete these sentences with the correct form of the verbs in brackets.

1. Ben hasn't come to the meeting. He _____ about it. (*must, forget*)
2. It's starting to rain. We _____ an umbrella. (*ought to, bring*)
3. Sorry I'm late. I _____ earlier. (*should, get up*)
4. What? You can't find your passport? You _____ it, can you? (*can't, lose*)
5. They lived in Paris for a year. They _____ a bit of French. (*could, learn*)
6. I can't find my dictionary. My brother _____ it. (*may, borrow*)
7. Joe is very late. He _____ (*might, oversleep*)
8. Sam was happy in London. If he hadn't lost his job, he _____ there. (*might, stay*)

4 Answer these questions. Work in pairs. Then share your ideas with the rest of the class.

1. A valuable statue is not in its place in the museum. What must have happened?
2. You can hear an ambulance siren. It is coming closer. What might have happened?
3. Mr and Mrs Jones visited London. They only saw Big Ben. What else could they have done?
4. During a football match the referee sent a player off the pitch. Why? What shouldn't the player have done?

Modal verbs + perfect infinitive

*I can't find my key. I **must have left** it at home.*
(= I believe I left it at home.)

*You **ought to** / **should have studied**.*
(= You had an obligation to study but you didn't.)

*The exam was hard. I **can't have passed** it.*
(= It is impossible that I have passed it.)

*You were there. You **could have said** something.*
(= It was possible to say something but you didn't.)

*I can't find John. He **may** / **might have gone** home.*
(= It is possible that he has gone home.)

*The boat sank? He **might have drowned**!*
(= Drowning was a possibility but he didn't drown.)

Grammar in use: modal verbs + perfect infinitive

Listening and speaking

Listening comprehension

1 🎧 **Listen to the festival committee meeting. Complete the chart with the correct names.**

music	art	dance and drama	literature
design of posters, etc.	refreshments	website and advertising	organising the helpers

2 🎧 **Read these questions. Then listen again and answer.**
1. Which student has made the chart?
2. Why are two people needed to organise the dance and drama programme?
3. Where does Vincenzo come from?
4. Why should Todd organise the website and the advertising?
5. How does Lucie feel about organising the music programme on her own?
6. What nationality is Marit?
7. Why does Ramon put her name forward?
8. Where is Zafira from?

3 Talk about it.
1. Do you think that the students are well-organised?
2. In your opinion, have they missed out any important details?

Individual speaking

You are going to talk about organising an event either in school or outside it.

Preparation in groups:
1. Think of an event which you have helped to organise.
   Perhaps it was a school event (e.g. a school play or show, open day for parents, a sports competition).
   Perhaps it was outside school (e.g. a birthday or anniversary party, a surprise party).
2. How many people were involved in organising the event? How did you decide what responsibilities everyone should have?
3. Describe in detail what you did to help.
4. Describe the event.
5. Was the event a success? Did anything go wrong?

Now tell the rest of the class about your group discussion. **WB p33**

Writing features

Story openings

> A **story opening** must make the reader interested enough to want to go on reading. Stories for young children are often very straightforward. Many begin by introducing the main characters and describing where they are: at home, in school, etc. Authors writing for an older audience often make the beginning of their stories more mysterious, leaving the reader with lots of unanswered questions.

Checklist
Look again at the opening of *Z for Zachariah* by Robert O'Brien on pages 30 and 31.

▸ **Plot / Structure**   The *plot* of a story is *what happens*. A straightforward story tells readers the things that happen, in the order that they happen. In this story, O'Brien begins in the *middle of the plot* and throughout the first few pages we learn something of what has happened *before*.
   Discuss:
   • what is happening in the story *now*.   • what has happened just *before now*.
   • what has happened *some time ago*.

▸ **Opening sentences**   The opening sentences of a straightforward story might be something like:
   Every Saturday, Mrs Brown took the twins, David and Sara to the market. After buying vegetables, they went to a café for something to drink. Nothing very mysterious about that!
   What are the first two sentences of O'Brien's story? Why are they mysterious? Why do you think he has opened his story like this?

▸ **Tenses**   Most stories are written in the past tense because they are relating what has happened in the past. O'Brien uses the past, present and future tenses.
   For what parts of the story does he use:
   • the past tense?   • the present tense?   • the future tense?
   Give an example of each tense from the extract.

▸ **Characters**   A story opening usually introduces readers to the main characters. We know their names and something about them very early on.
   Does this story begin in the usual way?
   What characters do readers meet in the opening of this story? Do we know their names? What do readers learn about them and what can they infer?

▸ **Person**   Stories can be written in the third person or the first person. In third person stories, the author is **not** one of the characters. In first person stories, the author tells the story from the point of view of one of the characters. The author is the narrator of the story.
   Is this a third or first person story? Why do you think O'Brien decided to write in this person?

▸ **Setting**   The setting of a story gives readers a picture of where the plot takes place. Usually the setting is described in detail but O'Brien doesn't do this. Readers have to pick up clues as to where the story is set.
   What do readers know and what can they guess about where the narrator is and what it is like? What do readers know about Ogdentown?

Writing assignment
You have read and discussed a mysterious opening for a story. You are now going to write your own mysterious opening in three paragraphs. Use present, past and future tenses. Write in the first person. Choose one of these as the first sentence of your story.

Go to p34 in your Workbook for help with your planning.

> I am excited.   I am worried.   I am unhappy.

It's a fact!

Start-up *Use WB p37 for your notes.*

Documentaries have different purposes …

▶ to inform and entertain

These tiny birds fly 6,000 kilometres every year, crossing two continents and two seas.

▲ to persuade viewers to a point of view by stating arguments and refuting opposite arguments

As prisoners forced to perform, these wild animals suffer huge stress. The idea that this is good entertainment for us and fun for them is far from the truth.

▲ to inform and advocate a point of view by presenting particular information in a particular way

The sea level will rise by seven metres and many coastal cities will be underwater.

What is a documentary?
Think of a documentary TV programme you have seen. What was it about?
Think of a documentary that has impressed you. Explain why.

Reading
- You will read a preview of a TV documentary. What is a *preview*? Do you read it before or after watching the programme?
- Next you will read a review of the TV documentary. What is a *review* and who writes it? When is it written?

Vocabulary
- These words are in the preview and review: *law   balanced (adj.)   procedure   apparently   outback   relieve*. Circle any you cannot remember or guess. Look them up.
- Find out what these phrases mean: *as a whole   well-being   life-threatening*.

Grammar
- You will study **non-defining relative clauses**. This type of clause adds extra information. What do you think is the extra information in this sentence? *My uncle, who is very kind, helped me with my science homework.*

Word focus
- Dictionary: You will look at **words with two or more meanings** for the same part of speech and other meanings as a different part of speech. Look up *run*. Find and count all the meanings.
- Spelling: You will look at the different spellings for the /əʊ/ sound. Write words for these spelling patterns: *o_e, ow, oa, ou*.
- Suffixes: You will look at the suffixes **-ology, -ist**. Think of a word ending with each suffix.

▶ **to give a balanced view and leave the viewer to decide**

Space exploration has cost billions but the benefits to mankind go far beyond the space programme itself.

◀ **to show other people's lives and to provide human interest**

This is Ashley's second term with the Cuban Ballet and things are even tougher.

▲ **to investigate matters of public concern**

In this programme we follow the trail of lies and excuses to find the source of the pollution.

▲ **to raise issues that ought to be a matter of public concern**

Every day 4,000 children die because they do not have access to clean water.

Grammar in use
- You will hear a discussion about the festival's dance and drama programme.
- You will study the use of the **third conditional**. Write example sentences for each of the other conditional structures.

Listening and speaking
- You will study and practise expressions used when agreeing and disagreeing. **Who do you agree with most often? Who do you usually disagree with?**
- You will ask for and give opinions in a group, then agree or disagree with different views.
- You will listen to part of a TV review programme. **Think of four different types of TV programme that it might review.**

Conversation focus 🎧 1.15
Kurt and Liam run the film club and they're tidying up after showing *West Side Story*.
1. Listen to their conversation about films and documentaries.
2. Read the questions on Workbook page 37. Listen again and answer the questions.
3. Talk in a group about different kinds of documentary films you like and / or have seen. Use the photos to help you, as well as any of your own ideas. Ask: *Did you see …? Why do you like / not like …?* Say: *I watched …, I prefer …*

Writing
- You will discuss the features of writing a review. A reviewer evaluates something. **What does *evaluate* mean?**
- You will write your own review of a television documentary. In a review you can praise what you like and criticise other parts. **Check you understand *praise* and *criticise*. What do you think you need to do while watching the programme you are going to review?**

39

Sharing the Planet: Animals in Science

Science Channel, **9.30pm**

Preview

Sharing the Planet is a five-part documentary showing how humans relate to the rest of the animal kingdom on planet Earth. The series as a whole looks at the exploitation of animals, and also the great lengths people go to to protect endangered species.

The programmes are presented by Professor Stan Collins, who is a leading expert in the field of zoology. He has travelled the globe investigating the different attitudes people have towards animals from ivory hunters in Africa, to projects which have been set up in the outback of Australia for the protection of kangaroos and wallabies.

In this first episode, *Animals in Science*, he concentrates on the use of animals in scientific experiments. He interviews the scientists who are convinced that these experiments are necessary and of huge value to the well-being of humans. He also talks to those who are opposed to using animals in this way and will go to great lengths – even breaking the law – to prevent it.

This programme, which is a serious investigation into the issue, contains some disturbing images and is not for the faint-hearted.

Last Night's TV
Sharing the Planet: Animals in Science
Science Channel, 9.30pm

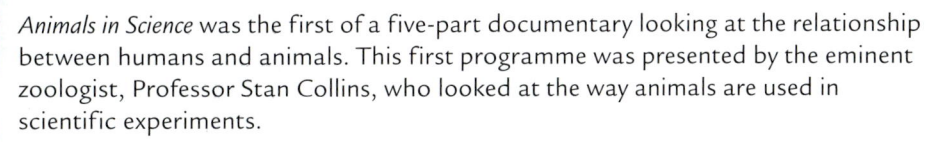

Review

Animals in Science was the first of a five-part documentary looking at the relationship between humans and animals. This first programme was presented by the eminent zoologist, Professor Stan Collins, who looked at the way animals are used in scientific experiments.

The documentary sets out to give viewers information about how and why animals are used in this way by talking to the scientists involved, and also examining the views of individuals and organisations opposed to the experiments.

Professor Collins was a skilled interviewer. When he spoke to people, he didn't bully them or try to put words in their mouth. I got the impression, however, that he was on the side of the scientists if their work was medical research but he had little time for those using animals to find a longer-lasting lipstick or a super-stay-on mascara. If the programme had spent more time investigating the use of animals in non-medical experiments, it would have been more balanced in my opinion.

I have always been aware that using animals in scientific experiments went on, though I didn't really know anything about it. The programme was very informative, explaining what actually happens and how it is regulated by law. I was interested to find out that scientists involved in this area follow the 'three Rs code'. This approach centres on: Replacement – replacing animal procedures with non-animal procedures wherever possible; Reduction – minimizing the number of animals used; and Refinement – improving the experiments so animals suffer as little as possible.

The programme did include some disturbing scenes of animals in high-tech labs and I, for one, felt very uncomfortable even though the scientists explained the crucial nature of the research for cancer and heart patients. Apparently, there are some experiments that cannot be done without animals.

Despite it being obvious that the programme makers wanted viewers to understand the need for animal testing, those opposed to it were given a voice. The main arguments were that animal testing can be misleading as an animal's response to a drug can be different to a human's; the stress that animals endure in labs can affect experiments, making the results meaningless; and that animals have as much right to life as human beings. They also said that the argument that animal testing relieves human suffering does not hold water when animals are still being used to test items like cleaning products. Unfortunately, Professor Collins did not ask the scientists to comment on that one!

The programme ended with Professor Collins speaking straight to camera. He posed the question: "If you or your loved ones could be saved from a life-threatening condition, would you refuse treatment if you knew that the drug or procedure was the result of animal experiments?" That's a tricky one for most of us but for those in the programme who saw an animal's right to life as equal to a human's, I think I know what the answer would be.

The programme was very interesting. It was based on thorough research and up-to-the-minute information and left viewers a lot to think about. As a non-scientist, I didn't feel that it went over my head, and I will certainly be watching the rest of the series.

Reading comprehension

1 Discuss these questions.

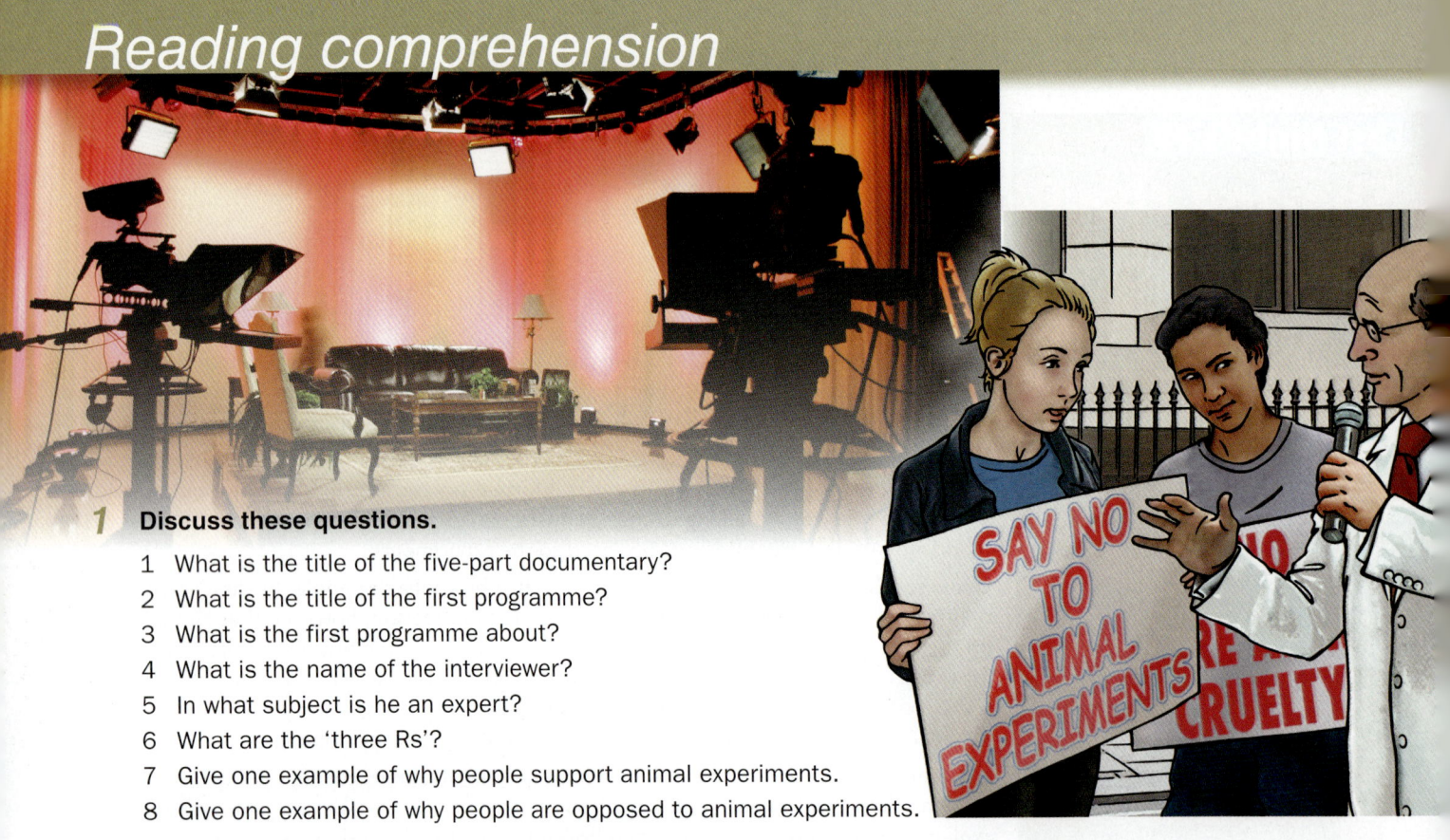

1. What is the title of the five-part documentary?
2. What is the title of the first programme?
3. What is the first programme about?
4. What is the name of the interviewer?
5. In what subject is he an expert?
6. What are the 'three Rs'?
7. Give one example of why people support animal experiments.
8. Give one example of why people are opposed to animal experiments.

2 Match the phrases to the correct definition as they are used in the reading texts.

1. faint-hearted
2. put words in their mouth
3. given a voice
4. does not hold water
5. went over my head

a brave
a lead them to say what he wants to hear
a told to be quiet
a is true
a difficult to understand

b easily upset
b ignore what they say
b allowed to speak
b is untrue
b easy to understand

3 Discuss these questions about the review.

1. What is the first heading on the review page?
2. What information does the reviewer give the reader in the first paragraph?
3. What does the reviewer explain in the second paragraph?
4. What is the reviewer's opinion of the presenter, Professor Stan Collins?
5. How much does the reviewer know about the subject?
6. How did the reviewer feel when the programme showed images of animals in 'high-tech' labs?

4 Discuss your answers to these questions.

1. What does the reviewer mean when she writes 'Professor Stan Collins was a skilled interviewer'?
2. Why do you think Professor Collins supports animal experiments for medical research but not for producing make-up?
3. What, in the reviewer's opinion, would have made the programme 'more balanced'?
4. Read the 'three Rs' again. Do you think these make animal experiments acceptable or not?
5. Read the arguments put forward by the people against animal experiments again. Do you agree or disagree with them?

5 What do you think?

Professor Stan Collins ends the programme by asking: "If you or your loved ones could be saved from a life-threatening condition, would you refuse treatment if you knew that the drug or procedure was the result of animal testing?". In groups, discuss your answer to this question.

Reading comprehension: literal, inferential and personal response questions; phrase definitions; reviews

Grammar

1 Read.

Animals in Science, **which was shown last night on the Science Channel**, was a documentary about animal testing. The programme was presented by Professor Stan Collins, **who is an eminent zoologist**. Professor Collins interviewed both scientists and members of the public, **many of whom were concerned about animal testing**. He also looked at recent medical advances, **most of which would not be available to patients if animal experiments had not taken place**. Some scenes were filmed in high-tech laboratories, **where animal experiments are frequently carried out**. There were some disturbing images but Professor Collins stressed that the way animals are treated today is much better than it was some years ago, **when there were fewer laws to protect animals**. The programme, **which was a serious investigation into the issue**, was shown late in the evening, **when young children would be in bed**.

2 Answer these questions.
1. What type of programme was *Animals in Science*?
2. Who did Professor Collins interview?
3. Where were some scenes filmed?
4. Are laws protecting animals better or worse today?
5. Why was the programme shown late in the evening?

3 Add the correct clauses in the correct position in the sentences.
1. *Animals in Science* was a fascinating programme.
2. It was presented by Professor Stan Collins.
3. The documentary was filmed in Manchester.
4. Amanda Jones was interviewed for the programme.
5. In 1984 Stan Collins became a professor of zoology.
6. *Sharing the Planet* will be broadcast over the next five weeks.

a. where there are several laboratories doing work of this kind
b. who works as a scientist in one Manchester lab
c. who is an eminent zoologist
d. which looks at the relationship between humans and animals
e. which dealt with animal testing
f. when he was only 24

4 Use your own ideas to complete the sentences.
1. Professor Collins spoke to members of the public, many of whom …
   Professor Collins spoke to members of the public, many of whom were against animal testing.
2. We watched several documentaries, most of which …
3. Professor Collins has two brothers, neither of whom …
4. There are 30 students in that class, half of whom …

5. Lucy borrowed five books from the library, none of which …
6. I enjoyed reading the novel, much of which …
7. John has nine cousins, one of whom …
8. These scientists perform experiments, some of which …

Non-defining relative clauses give us extra information about someone or something. If you remove the clause, the sentence will still make sense.
You can form non-defining relative clauses using *who* (for people), *which* (for things or animals), *where* (for places) and *when* (for times).
We met Lucy's father, **who is an opera singer**.
Tigers, **which were once a common sight**, are now rare.
Our next stop was Cairo, **where we visited the Pyramids**.
In 1967, **when John was four**, the family moved to Australia.
In some non-defining relative clauses, we use *whom* (for people) and *which* (for things or animals).
She has two sons, **both of whom are doctors**.
He collects stamps, **many of which are rare**.
Other similar phrases: *all of, any of, (a) few of, each of, either of, many of, most of, much of, none of, one / two / three of.*
A non-defining relative clause is always separated from the rest of the sentence by commas or a comma and a full stop.

Grammar: non-defining relative clauses

Word focus

A Dictionary work Words with two or more meanings (3)

Some words have two or more meanings for the same part of speech AND other meanings as a different part of speech.

- Dictionaries sometimes give the various meanings for the same part of speech in the form of word boxes.

field¹	/fiːld/	noun		
1 area for farming		4 space for information		7 area that can be seen
2 subject or type of work		5 where force has effect		
3 area for sport		6 area with gas, coal, etc.		

- The words in the word box will appear as entries to give you more information, e.g.

1 an area of land that is used for keeping animals or growing food: *a field of wheat*

field²	/fiːld/	verb	[T]	1 to catch or pick up the ball in sport
				2 to use a person or group of things as your representative or team

1 Use your dictionary. Which words can be used as a noun and a verb? A noun and an adjective?
  1 world   2 issue   3 human   4 programme   5 documentary   6 experiment

2 Choose three of the meanings for the noun *field* from the word box. Use each meaning in a sentence of your own.

B Spelling Words with the /əʊ/ sound

Words with the /əʊ/ sound can be spelled:
  o_e: wh**o**l**e**   oa: appr**oa**ch
  ow: kn**ow**n   ou: th**ou**gh

1 Write the o_e words for these definitions.
  1 against   o _ _ _ _ _ _ _
  2 shut   c _ _ _ _ _
  3 past tense of speak s _ _ _ _ _
  4 the world   g _ _ _ _ _
  5 part of a TV series e _ _ _ _ _ _ _

2 Complete these /əʊ/ words with **oa** or **ow**.
  1 tomorr _ _   2 c _ _ st
  3 s _ _ k   4 yell _ _
  5 s _ _ p   6 r _ _ d

C Word groups Television

Find three words in the preview and review that are to do with **television**.

D Suffixes *-ology* / *-ist*

Professor Stan Collins studies z**oology**.
The suffix *-ology* means 'the study of'.

1 Use your dictionary to find out what these subjects are the study of.
  1 bi**ology**   2 archae**ology**
  3 ge**ology**   4 anthrop**ology**

Professor Stan Collins is a z**oologist**.
The suffix *-ist* often tells us what somebody does, e.g. a person who studies z**oology** is a z**oologist**.

2 Who studies these subjects?
  1 bi**ology**   2 archae**ology**
  3 ge**ology**   4 anthrop**ology**

Grammar in use

1 🎧 Listen and read.

Rudi: Hi, Tasha! How's it going?
Tasha: Hi, Rudi! OK, I guess. Actually, I'm feeling a bit stressed.
Rudi: Why? What's up?
Tasha: It's the dance and drama programme. There's so much to do. To be honest, **if I had known how much work was involved, I wouldn't have taken it on.**
Rudi: Vincenzo's helping you, isn't he?
Tasha: Well, yes and no. He's just booked a Spanish dance troupe.
Rudi: That's great, isn't it?
Tasha: No! They're too expensive. We can't afford them. **I would've told him if he'd discussed it with me first.** I'll have to speak to Miss Jackson about it.
Rudi: Oh dear ... What about those Thai dancers you were talking about?
Tasha: No luck, I'm afraid. Someone else has booked them. I'm kicking myself. **If I had contacted them earlier, they could have taken part** but I left it too late.
Rudi: How about Eva Zemanova, that new Czech girl? She's an amazing ballet dancer.
Tasha: Really? You're not pulling my leg?
Rudi: No! She's absolutely brilliant. Didn't you know?
Tasha: No! **If someone had told me about her, I would have asked her straight away.** Why didn't you tell me, Rudi?

2 Answer these questions.

1. Why is Tasha feeling stressed?
2. What has Vincenzo done?
3. What should he have done?
4. Why is Tasha angry with herself?
5. How does Rudi solve Tasha's problem?

3 Find the correct endings. Write the letters.

1. If Tasha had contacted the Thai dancers earlier, ...
2. If someone had told Tasha about the Czech dancer, ...
3. If Tasha hadn't spoken to Rudi, ...
4. Tasha wouldn't have got cross with Rudi ...
5. A problem might have been avoided ...
6. The committee would not have booked *The River Boys* ...

a if she hadn't been so stressed.
b she would have contacted her immediately.
c if Vincenzo had spoken to Tasha.
d they could have taken part.
e if Gustav had had his way.
f she wouldn't have known about Eva.

4 Work in pairs. Think of your own endings for these sentences. Compare your ideas with the rest of the class.

1. If Henry had got up earlier, ...
2. If I had studied a little harder, ...
3. If they hadn't got stuck in a traffic jam, ...
4. I would have bought that jacket if ...
5. We would have been so happy if ...
6. John would have taken lots of photos if ...

We use the **third conditional** when we are thinking about the past and about something that did not happen. We are talking about unreal situations in the past.

*If I **had gone** to New York, I **would have seen** the Statue of Liberty.*
(But I didn't go to New York, so I didn't see the Statue of Liberty.)
If clause: past perfect (*had done*)
Main clause: conditional perfect (*would have done, could have done, might have done,* etc.)
The *If* clause can be placed first or second.
If he had studied harder, he would have passed.
He would have passed if he had studied harder.
Notice the short forms of the verbs:
If he'd studied harder, he would've passed.
If he'd studied harder, he'd've passed.

Grammar in use: third conditional **45**

Listening and speaking

Functions of English: agreeing and disagreeing

1 Look at these expressions.

Agreeing

> I agree.   I agree with you.   I think you're right.
> I think so, too.   You have a point there.   That's true.

Disagreeing

> I don't agree (with you).   I'm afraid I disagree.
> I'm sorry but I can't agree (with you).
> I don't think so.   I'm not so sure about that.

Partly agreeing

> Maybe you're right but …   I agree with you up to a point but …   That's not always the case.

Work in pairs. Read out these opinions. Agree, disagree or partly agree using the expressions above.

1 Watching TV is a waste of time.
2 Everyone should do some kind of sport.
3 Travel broadens the mind.
4 Football is boring.

2 Look at these expressions.

Expressing strong agreement

> Absolutely!   You're absolutely right!
> I totally agree.   I couldn't agree more.
> That's so true!   That's exactly how I feel.

Expressing strong disagreement

> I don't agree at all.   I totally disagree.
> I couldn't agree less.   No way!
> I'd say the exact opposite.   Nonsense!

Work in pairs. Read out these opinions. Agree or disagree strongly using the expressions above.

1 Playing computer games is a waste of time.
2 Girls are cleverer than boys.
3 Pop music is rubbish.
4 Cars should be banned from city centres.

3 Group conversation

Look back at Unit 2 page 24 and remind yourself how we ask for and give opinions.

Write three questions asking for opinions on any topic. Work in small groups. Ask and answer. Find out each other's opinions. Then agree or disagree using the expressions in the boxes above.

Listening comprehension

1 🎧 1.18 Listen to a conversation about a TV programme. Circle the correct answers.
1 What sort of programme was it?   a news   b TV preview   c TV review
2 How many people took part?   a two   b three   c four

2 🎧 1.18 Read the statements below. Listen again and write *T* (true), *F* (false) or *NS* (not stated).
1 Ashley Green is a ballet dancer from Britain. ....
2 He is 18 years old. ....
3 He is an only child. ....
4 He spent a year with the Cuban National Ballet. ....
5 Julie found the programme informative. ....
6 Peter thought Ashley complained too much. ....
7 Ashley speaks French, Italian, German and Swedish. ....
8 He learned Spanish before he went to Havana. ....
9 He found it difficult to make friends. ....
10 The family he stayed with were very kind to him. ....
11 Ashley trained six days a week. ....
12 Ashley will continue training with the Cuban National Ballet next year. ....

3 Discuss what you know about the documentary *Nine Months in Havana*. Would you have enjoyed it? Why? / Why not?

Writing features

A review

> A **review** is an article that gives the writer's opinion of a programme after it has been on air.
> The writer **evaluates** the programme.
> People who have watched the programme can agree or disagree with the reviewer's opinion.

Checklist
Look again at the review of *Sharing the Planet: Animals in Science* on page 41.

▸ **Title** It is important that the reader knows which programme is being reviewed.

   What is the title of the programme?
   What other information is given under the title?
   Why do you think this information is given?

▸ **Opening paragraph** In the *opening paragraph*, the reviewer gives the reader information about the documentary.

   What information is given in the opening paragraph of this review?

▸ **Purpose** The reviewer needs to be clear about the *purpose* of the documentary, so that he/she can judge it fairly.

   What does this documentary set out to do?

▸ **Presentation** Documentaries can be *presented* in different ways.
   - There may be a presenter who introduces the programme and is on screen for most of the time, interviewing people and explaining things to the viewers.
   - Sometimes the 'presenter' is just a voice that links the different parts of the documentary together.

   How is this documentary presented?

▸ **Reviewer's knowledge** Sometimes the reviewer is an expert in the subject of the documentary; sometimes they know very little about it.

   Is the reviewer of this documentary an expert or not? How do you know?

▸ **Content** A reviewer will summarise what the documentary was about.

   What did viewers learn about:
   - *what animal experiments are used for?*
   - *what code scientists follow?*
   - *what arguments those against animal experiments put forward?*

▸ **Reviewer's opinion** People who review programmes give their *opinion*.

   What opinion did the reviewer have of:
   - *Professor Collins as an interviewer?*
   - *Professor Collins' attitude to animal experiments?*
   - *the programme as a whole?*

Writing assignment
You have read and discussed a television documentary review. You are now going to write a review. Choose a documentary you can watch at home or at school. This may be in another subject, such as geography or science. Write a review explaining what the documentary was about and your opinion of it.

Go to p44 in your Workbook for help with your planning.

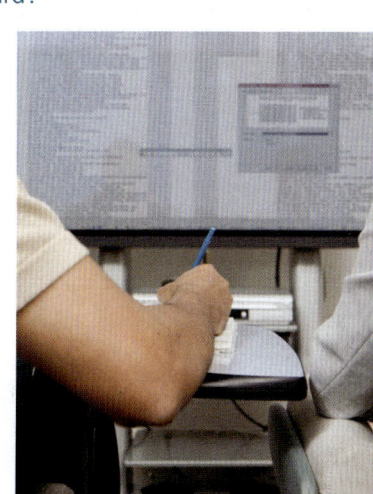

Life skills 1

Filling in forms

> There are lots of times when you need to **fill in a form**. You might want to join a club or organisation; apply for an educational course; volunteer for something.
> The thing to remember is that your form is the first impression that someone may get of you. It is worth taking the time and trouble to fill it in correctly.

Tips

▸ Always read through the whole form before you start to fill it in. This will help you to understand what information is needed and where it goes.

▸ If you are filling in the form by hand, make a photocopy and fill this in first, so you can check for mistakes before you fill in the actual form. If you can't make a photocopy, fill it in with a pencil first so you can rub out any mistakes.

▸ If you are filling the form in online, save it as you go along.

▸ Read all the instructions very carefully. Sometimes forms have to be completed in a special way. You may have to:
  - write in capitals, or use black ink.
  - fill in every part of the form. If something doesn't apply to you, you may be instructed to write *N/A* [not applicable].
  - write dates in a special way. For example: DD / MM / YYYY This means two numbers for the date and month, e.g. 01, 02, etc., and four numbers for the year, e.g. 2011.
  - tick a box or delete a word, e.g.
    Tick as appropriate: Mr ☐   Mrs ☐   Miss ✓   Ms ☐
    Delete as appropriate: ~~Mr~~   ~~Mrs~~   Miss   ~~Ms~~

▸ When you have completed the first draft of your form, get a friend or relative to check it before you fill in the actual form.

▸ Don't forget to sign and date your form.

▸ When you have completed the form, make sure you keep a copy.

The language of forms

These are some common words and abbreviations you will find in various forms. Match them to the correct definition.

| surname | forename | /cont | PTO |
| DoB | reference | nationality | employment |

1. .... date of birth
2. .... continued on next page
3. .... jobs
4. .... family name
5. .... country of birth
6. .... first name
7. .... please turn over
8. .... a written statement by someone who knows you well

Find the mistakes!

Here is a form filled in by someone who did not take much trouble to get it right.
Can you find all the mistakes?

[Complete the form in capitals and black ink. Use N/A where needed. Do not leave any gaps.] Delete as applicable:	
Mr ✓ Mrs Miss Ms	
Surname	Tom Wise
Forename	
Address	17, Park Street, London, England
Country	
DoB [DD/MM/YYYY]	6th July 1995
Nationality	Brittish

If you were receiving this form, what would it tell you about the person who filled it in?

About you

Some parts of a form require you to do more than tick, delete or write a few words.

Sometimes you need to explain in more detail why you are filling in the form.

Suppose you were filling in a form to join a sports club. The club is very popular but the people who run the club only want members who are very keen on sport and who want to improve and enter competitions.

The form tells you what sports the club offers and asks you to tick those you are interested in.

MEMBERS OF THE SPORTS CLUB CAN DO THE FOLLOWING SPORTS. PLEASE TICK THE ONE[S] YOU ARE INTERESTED IN.

SWIMMING ☐   TENNIS ☐   FOOTBALL ☐   DIVING ☐   SQUASH ☐

You are then asked to write a few sentences about why you want to be a member of the club, and how you think it will help you in your chosen sport.

EXPLAIN BRIEFLY WHY YOU WANT TO JOIN THE CLUB AND WHY YOU THINK BEING A MEMBER WOULD HELP YOU.

Discuss in groups how you would fill in this part of the form.

WB p118

Life skills 1: filling in forms

There's a problem

Start-up Use WB p49 for your notes.

▶ **Talk with your friends**
These might be friends at school or friends who live near you. They might be friends you don't see often but keep in touch with by phone, email or social network.

▲ **Talk it over at home**
You might want to ask your parents for advice. For help from a younger person, you might talk to a brother, sister or cousin. Grandparents may be useful to talk to. They can be more understanding than you expect.

▲ **Talk with a teacher**
You might want to talk to your class teacher. Alternatively, you could speak to another teacher who knows you well.

Who do you ask most often for advice when you have a problem?
Do you talk to a different person when you don't want advice but you want to know what someone else thinks?
What qualities are most important to you in the person or people you choose to talk to?
Is your choice of person changing as you get older? Might it change in the future?

Reading
- You will read a play script in which a serious issue arises in a school. A group of students discuss what to do about the problem. *Issue* sometimes means *problem* but it can have the same meaning as another word. Look in your dictionary and find the word.

Vocabulary
- These words are in the play script: cheat   clumsy   shove   deserve   shrug   devastate. Circle any you cannot remember or guess. Look them up.
- Find the meanings of these phrases. Write all the meanings that you find:
no trouble   (not) supposed to (have something)   in the making.

Grammar
- You will study **to be able to**. How old were you when you were able to read a whole book by yourself?

Word focus
- Dictionary: You will look at **example phrases and sentences** in a dictionary. Why are these included in a dictionary? Do you find them helpful? Why? / Why not?
- Spelling: You will look at different spellings with the /ɪɪ/ sound. Think of words of your own for these spelling patterns making the /ɪɪ/ sound: *ee, ea, ie, ei*.
- Suffixes: You will look at abstract nouns formed using suffixes *-ment*, *-dom*, *-ship* and *-ness*. What is an abstract noun?

5

▶ Discuss issues in a group
Some problems can be solved by a group such as a student council. Representatives meet especially to resolve particular kinds of issues that affect all students in the school.

▲ Problem-solving skills
The skills you need are much the same for any kind of problem, whether personal or not.
- be a good listener
- look at all sides of the issue
- think things through
- be ready to change your mind

▲ The International School festival committee
The students have solved problems and discussed some difficult issues. They are using a lot of skills to keep the group together and to make progress.

Grammar in use
- You will hear a discussion about the art and literature programme for the festival. What do you think could and should be included in the art and literature programme?
- You will study **reported questions with modal verbs**. Write down six modal verbs.

Listening and speaking
- You will listen to a presentation on the English artist, Henry Moore, who is best known as a sculptor. What does a sculptor do? List three kinds of materials a sculptor might use.
- You will prepare a presentation on an artist from your country.

Conversation focus 🎧 1.19
Florence and Giorgio have picked up forms for festival volunteers.
1. Listen to their conversation about taking part in the festival and the festival committee's work.
2. Read the descriptions on Workbook page 49. Listen again and write the name of the person.
3. Talk in a group about discussing problems, getting advice and problem-solving skills. Use the photos and short texts to help you, as well as any of your own ideas. Ask: *Who do you talk to …? What skills are most important …?* Say: *I talk to … because …, In problem-solving it's important to …*

Writing
- You will write the final scene of the play. Check that you understand these terms: scene   stage directions   action   lines   script   layout.

51

CHAMPION

Characters: Steven, Paul, Joe, Nina, Amy, Katie — school students

Scene 1: The locker room of the school sports centre. STEVEN is sitting on a bench putting things into his sports bag. PAUL jogs in.

STEVEN: Hey, Paul! That was a fantastic time you just did.

PAUL: Yeah, thanks *(breathlessly)*. Yeah, I was pleased with it.

STEVEN: Mr Hall was pleased with it, too. He said with a fast time like that, you ought to get a place in the national team, no trouble.

PAUL: Yeah … great. I mean, I hope so. But nothing's ever certain, is it?

[Paul takes his sports bag out of the locker and throws it onto the bench next to Steven. Steven moves over to make room for it.]

STEVEN: No … no, I suppose it isn't but I think you can be fairly confident. Well done.

PAUL: Thanks. *(takes towel out of locker and puts round his neck and dries his face)*

STEVEN: You deserve it. You've been training really hard all season.

PAUL: *(sits on bench and starts to take off trainers)* It's been tough, that's for sure. Still, no pain, no gain, eh?

STEVEN: *(laughs)* Maybe. But I don't seem to get anywhere for all my pain! No national team for me.

PAUL: You're improving, though.

STEVEN: Yes, but my results are nothing like yours. I'm just not as talented as you. *(pause)* By the way, I've brought in the CD of photos and the file of notes for the science project. Nina asked me if I could give them to you today. She was able to locate the last piece of information that we needed, so she wants you to finish your part by next week.

PAUL: Hmm, well, I'll try but I've got another practice session tomorrow. Oh, well, just put them on my bag, will you?

[Paul stands up and goes back to his locker. Steven puts a heavy folder on top of Paul's bag, which overbalances and falls off the bench and onto the floor. Objects fall out.]

PAUL: Clumsy!

STEVEN: Sorry! *(starts to pick things up)*

PAUL: It's OK, I'll do it! *(grabs things and stuffs them into his bag)*

STEVEN: Here, there's something under the bench.

[Steven picks up a small packet and looks at it.]

STEVEN: *(quietly)* What's this, Paul?

PAUL: Just something of mine. Here, give it to me.

STEVEN: But … you're not supposed to have these. No one is.

PAUL: What do you mean? Everyone does it.

STEVEN: No they don't. I don't.

PAUL: Yes, and look at your results. Do you want to be second best or do you want to be a champion?

STEVEN: *(shocked)* That isn't the choice, is it?

PAUL: Isn't it? Grow up, Steven.

[Paul grabs the packet out of Steven's hand and shoves it in his bag. Footsteps approach.]

Anyway, no need to say anything, is there? *(pauses and glares at Steven)* Is there?

[Joe enters.]

JOE: *(cheerfully)* Hi, guys! Fantastic time, Paul, brilliant! Champion in the making, eh, Steve? It's great for the school, isn't it? *(pause)* Hey, are you two OK? Nothing's the matter, is it?

Reading: a play script in two scenes

Scene 2: The school cafeteria, the next day.
STEVEN, JOE, NINA, AMY and KATIE are sitting round a table away from other students.

NINA:	So why didn't you say anything to anyone yesterday?
JOE:	I knew there was something wrong. It was written all over your face. Why didn't you tell me?
STEVEN:	I don't know. It felt like snitching, I suppose.
NINA:	Well, isn't this something you snitch about? It's cheating, Steven, it's plain cheating.
AMY:	I agree. I would have gone straight to Mr Hall and told him everything.
KATIE:	(*worriedly*) But think about it, Amy. What would happen to Paul?
JOE:	He'd be out of the school team and his dreams of the national team would be shattered.
AMY:	Well? What of it? He's cheated.
JOE:	But he lives for sport. His career would be dreadfully damaged. It might never be the same for him again.
AMY:	He should have thought of that before he started cheating and …
KATIE:	(*interrupting*) Look! I know he's done wrong. But shouldn't we talk to him about it first?
NINA:	And explain what he's done wrong? He's not a child. He knew what he was doing.
STEVEN:	Well, I'm not sure … It's just …
NINA:	Just what, Steven?
STEVEN:	It's just that I talked to him again … after you'd gone, Joe. I'm sure he didn't get into this on his own.
AMY:	How do you know? Did you ask him?
STEVEN:	(*sighs*) Well, no, not really. I just asked him why he needed to do it.
AMY:	And?
STEVEN:	(*shrugs*) He said he wanted to be the best.
AMY:	(*slaps the table impatiently*) Huh! I think we should tell Mr Hall.
JOE:	We're meeting him this afternoon anyway to finalise the programme for Sports Day.
AMY:	(*leaning forward*) If you don't tell him this afternoon, Steven, I will.
NINA:	(*firmly*) No, it has to be Steven.
STEVEN:	Mr Hall might not believe me.
JOE:	That's not a reason for not telling the truth, Steven.
KATIE:	But Paul was going to get the cup for outstanding achievement and …
NINA:	(*interrupting*) For goodness sake, Katie! We can't stand by and let the cup be presented to a cheat! That would be completely deceitful and I won't do it!
STEVEN:	But if I tell, everyone will know and he won't have a chance to put things right.
AMY:	OK, so does he want to put things right? Did you ask him if he would stop?
STEVEN:	Yes, I did but …
AMY:	(*pauses then speaks with irritation*) But what?
	[*Steven shakes his head.*]
AMY:	Well, then!
NINA:	Reporting him is the only thing that's going to stop him, can't you see that, Steven?
KATIE:	But reporting him is going to devastate his career.
JOE:	And think of the shame.
STEVEN:	I know we have to do something … but isn't there another way?

Reading: a play script in two scenes

Reading comprehension

1 Write the name of the person who said each line below. Write *P* (Paul), *S* (Steven), *K* (Katie), *N* (Nina), *A* (Amy) or *J* (Joe).

1 But nothing's ever certain, is it? ....
2 You deserve it. ....
3 You're improving, though. ....
4 Here, give it to me. ....
5 That isn't the choice, is it? ....
6 But think about it, Amy. ....
7 But he lives for sport. ....
8 He's not a child. ....
9 Did you ask him? ....
10 He said he wanted to be the best. ....
11 No, it has to be Steven. ....
12 I think we should tell Mr Hall. ....

2 Discuss these questions.

1 How many characters are in the play?
2 Which character is mentioned but does not appear?
3 How many scenes are there and where do they take place?
4 How many characters appear in Scene 1? How many appear in Scene 2?
5 Which scene has the most action? Find two examples of actions by characters.
6 In which scene are the characters' feelings shown most strongly? Find four examples of feelings in the scene you choose.

3 Discuss these questions about the characters.

1 In Scene 1, why do you think Steven was shocked when Paul asked him if he wanted to be second best or be a champion?
2 Read all of Paul's lines after Steven found the packet. What do you think Paul felt about being found out?
3 Why do you think Joe asked if anything was the matter?
4 In Scene 2, which two characters are strongly opposed to Paul? Why are they opposed?
5 Which two characters are uncertain about what to do? Why are they uncertain?
6 Which character is least keen on reporting Paul? Why?
7 Which of the characters do you agree with most? Which one do you agree with least?

4 Discuss your answers to these questions.

1 What happens to people who are found to have cheated in international sports competitions?
2 Why is cheating taken so seriously?
3 Do you agree that cheating should be taken seriously? Why? / Why not?
4 Can you think of any other situations where people might try to cheat?

5 What do you think?

- If you were sitting at the table with the students in Scene 2, what would you say about Paul?
- What would you suggest doing to try to solve the problem?
- Do you think it is easier or more difficult to solve serious problems by talking to your friends or by talking to a teacher?

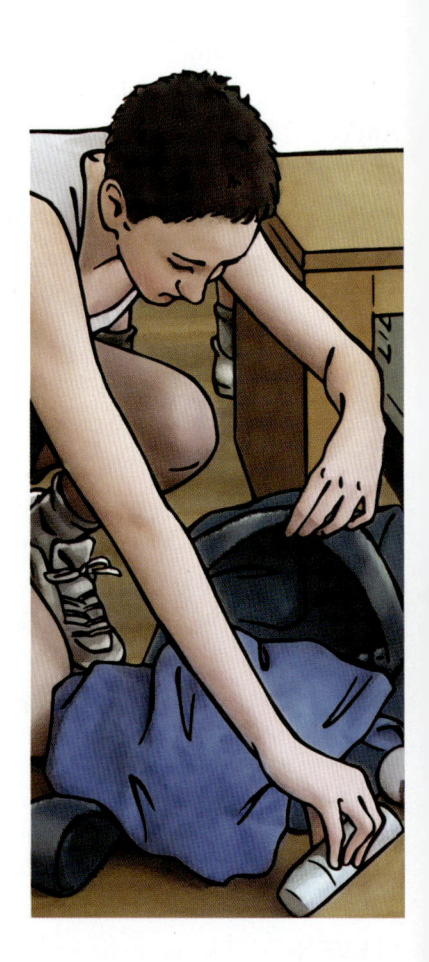

Grammar

1 **Read**

Paul has always been good at sport. He **was able to** swim when he was four and by the age of eight he was the star of the local swimming club. In races he **was** always **able to** beat the other boys. Swimming, football, basketball, tennis ... Paul excelled at all of them but these days his greatest passion is running. "I love it," he says. "I hope I**'ll be able to** turn professional one day."
In his last race, Paul was running against the best athletes in the area. It was a hard struggle but in the final seconds he **was able to** cross the finishing line first. His coach was delighted and told him that he **would** soon **be able to** get a place on the national team. "If you keep up the training, you **should be able to** do it." he said. However, recently Paul **has not been able to** achieve his previous fast times. He's worried about it. "I**'ve got to be able to** run faster," he says to himself. "What can I do ...?"

2 **Cover the text. Read the statements and write *True* or *False*. Correct the false statements.**

1 Paul was able to swim at a very early age.
2 He does not want to become a professional athlete.
3 His coach thinks he should be able to compete nationally.
4 Recently Paul has been running faster and faster.
5 He wants to be able to improve his times.

3 **Work in pairs. Use your own ideas to complete the sentences with *be able to*. Then compare your answers with the rest of the class.**

1 When I was four years old, I ...
2 If we go to the sports centre at the weekend, we ...
3 One day I would like ...
4 When my cousins went to New York, they ...
5 I always enjoy ...
6 If we were on holiday, we ...

4 **Read the following sentences. Where possible, replace *was / were able to* with *could*.**

1 In years gone by, many children were not able to go to school.
2 When my grandfather was a boy, he was able to swim in the river.
3 The path was steep but eventually the walkers were able to reach the top.
4 The students were not able to answer the question.
5 After making numerous phone calls, he was able to locate the missing laptop.
6 In the last minute of the match, our team was able to score the winning goal.

to be able to
to be able to expresses ability.
Present: *She **is able to** drive.*
(*can* is more common: *She **can** drive.*)
Past: *I **was able to** swim when I was four.*
(*could* has the same meaning: *I **could** swim when I was four.*)
Future: *He **will be able to** speak fluently soon.*
Present perfect: *I **haven't been able to** sleep.*
Past perfect: *They **had been able to** escape.*
Conditional: *If we had a car, we **would be able to** drive to school.*
Conditional perfect: *If you hadn't overslept, you **would have been able to** catch the train.*
Infinitive constructions: *He hopes **to be able to** study law.*
Gerund constructions: *I enjoy **being able to** travel.*
Modal constructions: *They **should be able to** survive.*
*He **must have been able to** buy it.*
was / were able to also describes an achievement in the past, something that was successfully completed.
*The violent storm was terrifying but eventually the ship **was able to** reach the safety of the harbour.*
(Here it means the same as *managed to* or *succeeded in*. It does not have the same meaning as *could*.)

Grammar: *to be able to* **55**

Word focus

A Dictionary work Example phrases / sentences

Dictionaries often give an *example phrase or sentence* to show how a word is used in context.

| national | /ˈnæʃ(ə)nəl/ | adjective | 1 relating to one particular nation: *the national and international news* |
| | | | 2 relating to the whole of a nation: *House prices in the capital city are 5% higher than the national average.* |

1 Find an example phrase or sentence in the dictionary for these words from the play script.
   1 fantastic   2 confident   3 locate

2 Write a simple phrase or sentence that could be used in a dictionary definition to show the meaning of these words in context.
   1 tough   2 results   3 career

B Spelling Words with the /iː/ sound

Words with the /iː/ sound can be spelled:
   ee: s**ee**m   ie: bel**ie**ve
   ea: pl**ea**sed   ei: dec**ei**tful

1 Complete these /iː/ words with *ee* or *ea*.
   1 ch __ __ t   2 n __ __ d
   3 m __ __ ting   4 dr __ __ ms
   5 t __ __ m   6 s __ __ son

2 Complete these /iː/ words with *ei* or *ie*.
   1 p __ __ ce   2 rec __ __ ve
   3 dec __ __ ve   4 ach __ __ ve
   5 c __ __ ling   6 br __ __ f

3 There are a few words that have the /iː/ sound made by e_e. Write the e_e words for these definitions.
   1 opposite of *those*   t __ __ __ __
   2 part of a play   s __ __ __ __
   3 whole   c __ __ __ __ __ __ __

C Word groups Sport

Find five words or phrases in the play script that are to do with **sport**.

D Suffixes -ment / -ness / -ship / -dom

Adding the suffix *-ment* to some verbs forms an abstract noun, e.g.
achieve → achieve**ment**

1 Add *-ment* to each of these verbs to form an abstract noun.
   1 embarrass   2 excite
   3 move   4 govern
   5 improve   6 encourage

2 Use four of the abstract nouns you have formed in sentences of your own.

Abstract nouns can also be formed with the suffixes *-ness*, *-ship* and *-dom*.

3 Form abstract nouns by adding the correct suffix to these words. Use your dictionary to help you.
   1 bore   2 dark
   3 friend   4 member
   5 wise   6 cheerful
   7 owner   8 free

4 Use four of the abstract nouns you have formed in sentences of your own.

56 Word focus: dictionary work; spelling; word groups; suffixes

Grammar in use

1 🎧 Listen and read.

Ramon: Hi, Rudi! Did I see you talking to Miss Jackson?
Rudi: Yes. We were having a chat about the art programme. **She was wondering where we should put the sculpture exhibition.**
Ramon: Can't it go in the hall or in the foyer?
Rudi: No. The hall's booked for dance and drama and music. And we've got the painting exhibition in the foyer.
Ramon: Oh, right. That's a bit tricky.
Rudi: Well, **Miss Jackson wanted to know whether the sculpture exhibition had to be indoors. She wondered if the sculptures might go outside.**
Ramon: That sounds like a brilliant idea.
Rudi: Yes, I think so. How's your literature programme coming along?
Ramon: OK, I think. We've got a poetry competition and story-telling for children. And, of course, Eliza Brodie is coming.
Rudi: Really? *The* Eliza Brodie? The famous author? Wow!
Ramon: I'm just going to email her, actually.
Rudi: And I'm going to phone Professor Barnes, our eminent archaeologist. **He asked if I could let him know how big his audience might be.**
Ramon: It'll be huge, I bet. He's really popular. Hey! Where on earth are you going to put him?

2 Answer these questions.

1. Why was Rudi having a chat with Miss Jackson?
2. What did she suggest?
3. Which programme is Ramon responsible for?
4. Who is his star speaker?
5. Why is Professor Barnes likely to have a big audience?

3 Report these questions.

1. "Should I speak to Miss Jackson?"
   Tasha asked Todd ...
2. "Ought we to have the exhibition outside?"
   Miss Jackson wondered ...
3. "Might Professor Barnes get a big audience?"
   Lucie wanted to know ...
4. "When do we have to interview the volunteers?"
   Rudi asked ...
5. "Where may the spectators sit?"
   Gustav asked ...
6. "Why must you email Eliza Brodie?"
   Lucie asked Ramon ...

4 Look at these reported questions from the text. What were the original direct questions?

1. She was wondering where we should put the sculpture exhibition.
2. Miss Jackson wanted to know whether the sculpture exhibition had to be indoors.
3. She wondered if the sculptures might go outside.
4. He asked if I could let him know how big his audience might be.

Reported questions with modal verbs

When the reporting verb is in the past tense, some modal verbs change in reported speech.

"**Must** we leave?" →
He asked if we **had to** leave.
"Do you **have to** go?" →
I wanted to know if they **had to** go.
"**Can** I help you?" →
She asked whether she **could** help me.
"Where **may** I sit?" →
She wondered where she **might** sit.

Some modal verbs do not change:
"What **should** I say?" →
He asked what he **should** say.
These verbs do not change: *should, ought to, might.*
When reporting questions, you can use *if, whether* or a question word.
There are no question marks at the end of reported questions.
Be very careful about word order!

Grammar in use: reported questions with modal verbs

Listening and speaking

Listening comprehension

1 🎧 **Listen to part of a talk about Henry Moore. Then answer these questions.**
  1. What was Henry Moore's nationality?
  2. What is he most famous for today?

2 🎧 **Listen again and choose the best answer.**
  1. Henry Moore was born in ...
     a the 19th century.   b the 20th century.   c the 21st century.
  2. His family was ...
     a rich.   b poor.   c small.
  3. The first person to notice his artistic talent was ...
     a his mother.   b his father.   c his teacher.
  4. When Moore decided to become an artist, his parents were ...
     a delighted.   b disappointed.   c angry.
  5. Moore's wife was from ...
     a London.   b Yorkshire.   c Russia.
  6. His abstract sculptures were inspired by ...
     a his studio.   b natural objects.   c the beach.
  7. He started making his family group sculptures ...
     a before his mother died.   b before his daughter was born.   c after his daughter was born.
  8. The figures in his sculptures of women are usually ...
     a sitting or lying down.   b standing.   c running or jumping.
  9. Moore earned ... from his art.
     a a great deal of money   b very little money   c no money
  10. Moore influenced ...
      a a few sculptors.   b many sculptors.   c no sculptors.

3 Talk about it.

Look at this work by Henry Moore. Describe it.
What do you think of it?

Individual speaking

You are going to talk about an artist from your country.
Preparation in groups:
  1. Think of artists (painters and sculptors) from your country. Make a list.
  2. What do you know about them?
  3. Where can you see their work?
  4. Can you describe any of their paintings or sculptures?
  5. Do you like or dislike any of these works? Why?

Now tell the rest of the class about your group discussion.

WB p55

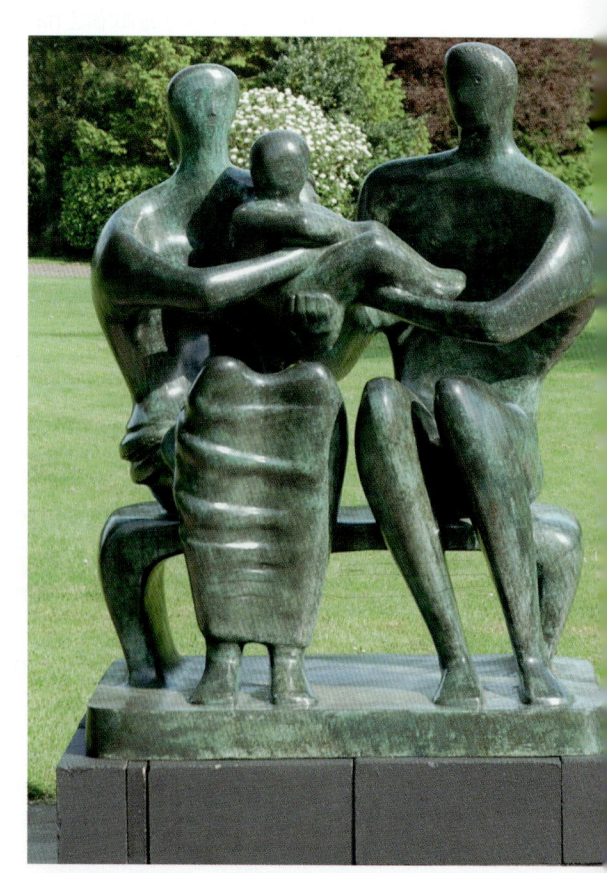

58 Listening and speaking: listening comprehension: monologue; individual speaking: an artist from your country

Writing features

Writing about issues

> In fiction – stories, plays and poems – writers often use real life issues. The characters find themselves in difficult situations and have to make choices. In the play script extract you have read, Steven discovers that Paul is cheating. What is he going to do? He tells his friends but they cannot agree. Should they tell the teacher or not? This part of the play is called the 'dilemma'.

Checklist
Look again at the play script *Champion* on pages 52 and 53.

▶ **Characters** — A play script begins with a list of the characters.
   Who are the characters in the play?

▶ **Scene** — Plays can have any number of scenes. Sometimes scenes are grouped together as 'Acts'.
   How many scenes are in the play? Where does each scene take place?

▶ **Layout** — A play script is set out in a very particular way.
   Where will you always find the characters' names?
   How are they written? Where will you always find the dialogue?

▶ **Stage directions** — There are two main types of stage direction.

1. Stage directions on the same line as the dialogue are in italics and round brackets. These show how a character says the words and what he/she does when speaking, e.g. Yeah, thanks (*breathlessly*). Yeah, I was pleased with it.
2. Stage directions that appear on a new line and centred under the dialogue are in italics and square brackets. These show what characters do when not speaking, e.g.

   [*Steven picks up a small packet and looks at it.*]

   Find two more examples of each type of stage direction in the play script.

▶ **Dialogue** — Dialogue is what the characters say. The writer uses various ways to make the speech seem realistic.

1. Sometimes a character does not finish a sentence, e.g.
   STEVEN: Well, I'm not sure … It's just …
   NINA: Just what, Steven?
2. Sometimes a character is interrupted, e.g.
   AMY: He should have thought of that before he started cheating and …
   KATIE: (*interrupting*) Look! I know he's done wrong. But shouldn't we talk to him about it first?
3. Sometimes a character says only one word, e.g. **PAUL:** Clumsy!

   Find one other example of each of these types of realistic speech in the play script.

▶ **Characters through dialogue** — Dialogue is also important because it tells us what sort of person each character is and what they think.

   The issue in the play script is that Paul is cheating. Take each character in turn and explain what their attitude is to what Paul has done. Quote something they say to support your views.

▶ **Action** — This is what happens in the scenes, like the plot in a story.
   Summarise what happens in the two scenes.

Writing assignment
You have read the first two scenes of a three-scene play. You are now going to write the final scene.
Either: The group decide they need to talk to Paul and sort it out between themselves.
Or: They report Paul to Mr Hall and the teacher talks to him.
Or: Think of your own idea.

Go to p56 in your Workbook for help with your planning.

Sounds amazing – let's go!

Start-up Use WB p59 or your notes.

▼ Travel articles are popular and they often appear in magazines. They usually give the reader a broad picture of a fairly well-known place through a recount from personal experience.

▲ Some magazines are produced especially for people interested in travel. The places in the articles may be more unusual.

▼ Travel books give a detailed picture of a place or region. They often tell the story of a journey and describe sights and experiences precisely. The author might be in the photos.

Where have you travelled to in the past?
Are you interested in travelling in the future? Why? / Why not?
Do you prefer to watch programmes about other places instead of going there yourself? Why?
If you would like to travel in the future, what kind of destinations would you choose?

Reading
- You will read a travelogue from a magazine. Is a travelogue fiction or non-fiction?
- The writer has won an award for her travel writing. What is *an award*?

Vocabulary
- These words are in the travelogue: *vibrant   splendour   conquer   aspiration   ambition   prominent*. Circle any you cannot remember or guess. Look them up.
- Find out what these phrases mean: *to take your life in your hands   shop until you drop*.

Grammar
- You will study the **future perfect simple**. Have you got homework today? What homework will you have done by tomorrow morning?

Word focus
- Dictionary: You will look at **Grammar boxes** in a dictionary. They help with common mistakes in using words. Do you know when to use *much* instead of *a lot of*?
- Spelling: You will look at words ending *-le*, *-el*, *-al*. Think of one word you already know for each ending.
- Prefixes: You will look at the negative prefix *ir-*. Think of two words beginning with other negative prefixes.

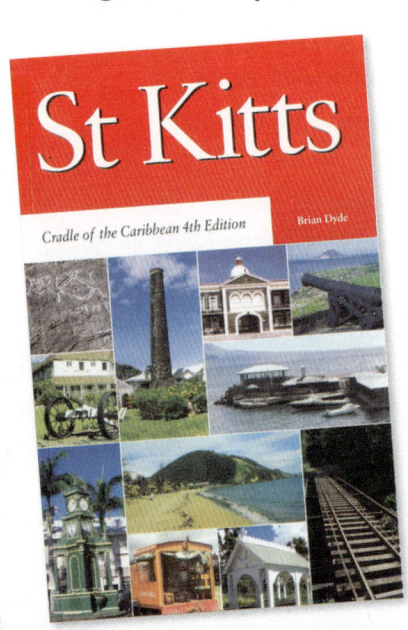

▼ Many people enjoy travel programmes on TV. They find out about places they may never go to and share some of the experiences of the programme's presenter.

▲ On the internet, people post their own travel experiences, advice and pictures. If you search for almost any building or destination, you will find hundreds of images taken by travellers all around the world.

Grammar in use
- You will hear a discussion about the festival music programme. **Think of four different kinds of music that the students plan to include.**
- You will study **defining and non-defining relative clauses** and **relative clauses with *whose*** and compare the two types of clause. **Think of three other words that often begin a relative clause.**

Listening and speaking
- You will learn and practise expressions for making, accepting and refusing offers. **Think of a situation when you offered to do something for someone. Did he/she accept or refuse?**
- You will listen to conversations in which people offer to help others. **Think of a situation when someone offered to do something for you. Did you accept or refuse?**

▼ Some newspapers include travel articles about places in the news. If a lost city was discovered, a writer might describe going to see it.

Conversation focus 🎧 2.01
Liam and Kurt are in the library. Liam is online. Kurt is looking at magazines.
1. Listen to their conversation about travelling to other places. Find some of the places in the photos.
2. Read the questions on Workbook page 59. Listen again and answer the questions.
3. Talk in a group about travelling to different destinations. Use the photos to help you, as well as any of your own ideas. Ask: *Where would you like to …? Why? How would you get to …?* Say: *I want to go to … because …, I don't want to go to … because …*

Writing
- You will write your own travel article that is a personal account. It will be about a place you have been to and that you know well from your own experience. **Will you write the article in the first person or third person?**

Karen Rivers, winner of the Young Travel Writer Award, gives her personal view of a city to which she is a frequent visitor.

Istanbul – a city of two continents

At the eastern end of Europe, where it is separated from Asia by a short, narrow channel of water, there is a vast and fascinating city. On either side of the Bosphorus stands Istanbul, the largest city in Turkey and one of the largest cities in the world. Sometimes called The Paris of the East and The City of the Seven Hills, this vibrant city, where ancient and modern stand side by side, has for centuries been known as a crossing point where East meets West.

So narrow is the Bosphorus that it seems more like a river running through a great city. Take a boat trip along it and you'll see houses, cafés, hotels and restaurants crowding down to the water's edge on either side of you. You would never guess that the two suspension bridges spanning the channel link two continents. You would never guess that the Bosphorus connects two great seas: the Black Sea and the Aegean.

The European side is the older part and the financial district is on that side, too. Land and houses are expensive, so lots of residents live in Asia and work in Europe. If you live in Istanbul, just going to work or college can mean changing continents twice a day. I've always found it one of the most fascinating aspects of the city. Unfortunately, there is no road tunnel under the Bosphorus. The bridges get completely clogged with vehicles during the rush hour and the ferries are crowded. Perhaps the city's commuters don't find changing continents quite so fascinating.

Traffic is one of my least favourite things about Istanbul and the roads are far too busy for my liking. In the large and bustling Taksim Square, you take your life in your hands when you walk across. Cars approach dangerously fast from all directions, horns blaring and smelling like old oil cans. Fortunately, there are plenty of areas in the city where there is little or no traffic at all, so whether you want to shop until you drop, view the historic sites or relax in a courtyard café, there's somewhere that will be just right for you.

In Istanbul, you can't ignore the history. Its magnificent structures are of real architectural splendour and a visual inspiration, especially if you have a camera to hand. By the end of your visit, you will have taken hundreds of stunning photos. The domes and soaring arches of the Hagia Sofia impress every visitor. This church, which became a mosque and is now a museum, was built 1,500 years ago. I find it truly uplifting and it's one of my favourite buildings. The city itself was established a thousand years earlier, by King Byzas, for whom it was named Byzantium. So it continued for 900 years until conquered by the Roman Emperor, Constantine, and renamed Constantinople. Sultan Mehmed II, whose armies besieged and captured the city more than 500 years ago, made it the capital of the Ottoman Empire, which lasted until the Republic of Turkey was established by Kemel Ataturk in 1923. The city became known by its old name of Istanbul. Ankara, which is in central Turkey, became the capital of the new Republic.

With such a long and varied history of empire, power and ambition, it is not surprising that Istanbul has such a wealth of palaces, churches, mosques, towers and fortresses with which to dazzle any visitor. The most well-known, the Topkapi Palace, the Hagia Sofia and the Sultan Ahmed Mosque are all close to each other in the old part of the city so you can visit them all in a day.

History may be all around you in Istanbul but one of the best things about the city today is its modern outlook. The average age of its population is 23, so it's a city of young people with ideas and aspirations. It has a new modern art museum and hosts an annual international film festival, music and opera festivals, ballet and theatre. During the long hot summer the city's many cafés and restaurants are cool oases in which to meet and chat. They still buzz with life on winter days when one of Istanbul's frequent fogs descends or a heavy snowfall covers the streets.

For anyone whose passion is shopping, Istiklal Avenue has everything you could want to buy and more. This three-kilometre, pedestrianised street is said to attract a million visitors a day but I'm not fond of it. International brands are rather too prominent. My favourite place to shop and eat out is the Grand Bazaar. It's the oldest covered market in the world. To me, it's irresistible, like a giant Aladdin's cave – beautiful and full of treasures. That's not a bad way to describe the whole city. There's something wonderful round every corner. If you get the chance, go and see for yourself.

Reading comprehension

1 Scan the text to find the answers to these questions.
1. What is the name of the narrow channel of water that separates the two parts of the city?
2. Which two seas are joined by this channel?
3. Which square does the writer say is dangerous for pedestrians?
4. What was the city's first name?
5. Which Roman conquered the city?
6. What was the city's next name?
7. Who captured the city and made it the capital of the Ottoman Empire?
8. Who established the Republic of Turkey in 1923?
9. What is the name of the main shopping street in modern Istanbul?
10. Where does the writer prefer to shop and eat out?

2 Read the phrases 1–5. Read the definitions a–e.
Complete the definitions with the words from the box. Match them to the phrases 1–5.

1 side by side ....
2 rush hour ....
3 for my liking ....
4 to take your life in your hands ....
5 to shop until you drop ....

| next | taste | exhausted | morning | dangerous | buying | home | evening | work |

a the time early in the .... when people are travelling to .... and the time in the .... when they are going .... again
b to do something .... that could cause death
c to spend a lot of time in the mall choosing and .... lots of things until you are too .... to go on
d .... to something else
e for my ....

3 Discuss your answers to these questions.
1. Why do you think Istanbul has been fought over and captured so often?
2. Why do you think Karen Rivers dislikes the international brands being prominent in Istiklal Avenue? Do you think international brands are a good thing or not?
3. Which information in the article do you think gives you the best idea of what the city is like?
4. Karen Rivers has won an award for her writing. Do you think this is a good article? What do you like about it?

4 What do you think?
- Does reading the article make you want to visit Istanbul? Why? / Why not?
- Which of these aspects of the city would you like to know more about: history and architecture, arts events and performances, shopping and street life? Why?
- Out of all the places in Istanbul that Karen Rivers mentions, which would you like to go to? Why?

Grammar

1 Read.

Ollie Johnson is a history student with a passion for travel. One of the places that he has always wanted to visit is Istanbul. Travelling can be expensive and, as a student, Ollie does not have a lot of money but he has been saving money and also working in the university holidays. By next summer he **will have saved up** enough money to pay for his trip.

He has been reading about the city and looking at pictures on the internet. By the time he leaves for Turkey next July, he **will have planned** his trip down to the last detail. He is longing to see Istanbul's mosques, palaces and fortresses, especially Hagia Sofia and the Topkapi Palace. He wants to take a boat trip along the Bosphorus, and he can't wait to eat out and shop for souvenirs at the Grand Bazaar.

By the time he returns in August, he **will have visited** two continents, Europe and Asia, and **been dazzled** by the sights and sounds of this remarkable city. By the time he gets home, he **will have had** the holiday of a lifetime.

2 Cover the text. Correct these sentences.

1. By next spring Ollie will have saved up enough money for his trip.
2. By the time he leaves for Spain, he will have planned his trip down to the last detail.
3. By the time he comes home, he will have visited three continents.
4. He will have been dazzled by the sights and sounds of Ankara.
5. He will not have had a very good holiday.

3 Complete these sentences with verbs from the box. Use the future perfect simple.

be	spend	write
read	travel	leave

1. By the time he reaches his destination, he .... a thousand miles.
2. Jane .... her essay by lunchtime.
3. By November all the tourists ....
4. By the time Ollie gets home, ... he .... all his money?
5. On 6th August my grandparents .... married for 40 years.
6. I'm afraid I .... not .... the novel before our next class.

4 Think about it. Make notes. Then ask and answer in pairs.

What will you have done …
1. by this time tomorrow?
2. before next summer?
3. by the time you take your next exams?
4. by the time you are 25?

What won't you have done …
1. by the end of school today?
2. before next week?
3. before the end of term?
4. by the time you are 18?

Future perfect simple

We use this tense when we are thinking about an action which will be completed before another action or a time in the future.
Formation: *will* + *have* + past participle
By the time you read this letter, I **will have left** *the country.*
By next summer they **will have finished** *building their house.*
We also use this tense when we are thinking about a continuous action before a time or event in the future.
By next July I **will have known** *my best friend for ten years.*
When he retires, Mr Johns **will have taught** *at this school for 35 years.*
You can often use *be going to* instead of *will*.
By next July I **am going to have known** *my best friend for ten years.*
Always use the present tense in time clauses.
By the time he **gets** *home, he* **will have visited** *20 countries.*

Grammar: future perfect simple

Word focus

A Dictionary work Grammar boxes

Grammar boxes give extra information to help you learn more about how a word is used and how to avoid common mistakes.

ago /əˈgəʊ/ adverb   used for saying how much time has passed since something happened: *How long ago did this happen?*

- Use **ago** to say how long before the present time something happened: *He died two years ago.*
- Use **before** to say how long before a time in the past something happened: *I remembered that I had met her ten years before.*
- Use **for** to say how long something in the past continued: *They were married for almost 30 years.*

it's / its
1 Look up the word *its* in your dictionary.
2 Read the Grammar box.
3 Write a sentence using *it's* and a sentence using *its* to show you understand the information in the Grammar box.

little / a little
1 Look up the word *little* in your dictionary.
2 Read the Grammar box.
3 Write a sentence using *little* and a sentence using *a little* to show you understand the information in the Grammar box.

B Spelling Words ending in *-le*, *-el* and *-al*

-le is the most common ending, e.g.
litt**le**   dazz**le**

1 Write the *-le* words for these clues.
   1 physically weak   f e _ _ _ _
   2 speak quietly   m u _ _ _ _
   3 frighten or surprise s t _ _ _ _ _

-el is the least common ending, e.g.
chann**el**   tunn**el**

2 Use these *-el* words in sentences of your own.
   1 cruel   2 hotel   3 quarrel

Some nouns end in *-al*, e.g.
mamm**al**   festiv**al**
-al is also a suffix that makes a noun into an adjective, e.g.
architecture → architectur**al**
centre → centr**al**

3 Write the *-al* adjectives from these nouns.
   1 nation   2 industry   3 origin
   4 myth   5 nature   6 music

C Word groups Buildings and transport

1 Write the headings: **buildings**   **transport**
   Find four words for each group from the article.
2 Put each word group into alphabetical order.

D Prefixes *ir-*

Adding the prefix *ir-* makes a word into its opposite, e.g. *To me, it's **ir**resistible, like a giant Aladdin's cave.*
resistible → **ir**resistible

1 Add the prefix *ir-* to these words to form their opposites.
   1 responsible   2 rational
   3 relevant   4 regular

2 Use a dictionary to make sure you understand the meaning of each opposite you have formed.

3 Use each opposite you have formed in Activity 1 in a sentence of your own.

4 Match each of these *ir-* words with the correct definition.
   irreparable   irreversible   irreplaceable
   1 impossible to change   2 impossible to replace
   3 impossible to mend

Grammar in use

1 🎧 Listen and read.

Todd: So, Lucie, what's happening with the music programme?
Lucie: Well, tickets for the pop concert went on sale this week and we've sold loads.
Todd: I'm not surprised. *The River Boys* are so popular. Any other news?
Lucie: Well, you'll really love the jazz band **that we've found**. They're brilliant and, what's more, they come from Bay City, **which is only a few kilometres away**, so we won't have to pay for their travelling expenses.
Rudi: Good work, Lucie!
Todd: What about traditional music?
Lucie: Well, Zafira and I have made a list of students **who can perform traditional music**.
Rudi: Zafira?
Lucie: She's the girl **whose parents own the Lebanese restaurant in town**.
Rudi: Oh, right. The girl **that's helping you organise the refreshments**.
Todd: What about the classical concert?
Lucie: Well, we've booked Gustav's uncle's orchestra and they're going to play Mozart.
Tasha: I was talking to Gustav the other day and guess what? Gustav, **who was so against putting on a pop concert**, has been listening to a *River Boys'* CD.
Rudi: You're joking!
Tasha: It's true! And he likes them so much that he's bought a ticket for their concert!

2 Answer these questions.

1. Have tickets for the pop concert sold well? Why?
2. Where does the jazz band come from? Why is this good?
3. What sort of list has Lucie made?
4. What do you know about Zafira?
5. What has Gustav done? Why is this surprising?

3

> We use *whose* in relative clauses to show possession.
> She found a jazz band. Their music is excellent.
> She found a jazz band **whose music is excellent**.

Join these sentences using *whose*.

1. Gustav is the student. His uncle is a conductor.
2. That is the old lady. Her house is by the lake.
3. Those are the students. Their exam results were the best.
4. The man is angry. His car was damaged.
5. The girl is upset. Her cat was stolen.
6. The four students must retake the exam. Their results were poor.

4

> **Defining relative clauses** give information which is necessary to understand the meaning of a sentence.
> There's a book on the chair and a book on the desk. Which one do you want?
> I want the book **which is on the desk**.

> You can start these clauses with *who*, *which*, *that*, *whose*, *where* and *when*.
> Don't use commas with these clauses.
> **Non-defining relative clauses** give extra information which is not necessary to understand the meaning of a sentence.
> *I have one old book. This book,* **which was written in 1875**, *was given to me by my dad.*
> You can start these clauses with *who*, *which*, *whose*, *where* and *when* (but not *that*).
> Always use commas with these clauses.

Read these sentences. Underline the relative clauses and write D (defining) or ND (non-defining).

1. She saw the boy who had stolen her mobile. ......
2. The film which we saw last night was superb. ......
3. Gustav, whose uncle is a conductor, comes from Germany. ......
4. Charles Dickens wrote his novels in the 19th century, when Queen Victoria was on the throne. ......
5. The holiday that we had last year was great. ......
6. Paris, where Lucie was born and brought up, is a popular tourist destination. ......

5 Look at the dialogue in Activity 1 above. Say if the relative clauses are defining or non-defining.

Listening and speaking

Functions of English: offering to do something; accepting or refusing an offer of help

1 **Look at these useful expressions.**

> Can I …?   Shall I …?   Let me …   Would you like me to …?   I'll / I can … if you want / like.
> Would you like some / any help with …?   Do you need some / any help with …?   Is there anything I can do (to help

Read the following situations. Offer to help using the expressions in the box above.
1 It is very hot in your classroom.
2 Your friend's room is very untidy.
3 You see an elderly lady trying to carry a heavy suitcase.
4 Your mum is busy preparing dinner.

2 **Work in pairs. Look at these expressions for accepting and refusing help.**

> **Accepting help**
> Thank you (very much).   Thanks (a lot).
> Yes, please.   If you're sure it's no trouble.
> That's / That would be very kind (of you).
> I'm / would be very / most grateful.

> **Refusing help**
> No, thank you / thanks.   No, really.
> That's very kind of you but …   No, don't worry.
> I can manage, thanks.

Read out these offers of help. Accept or refuse help.
1 Shall I help you revise for the exams?
2 Let me carry your books for you.
3 Would you like me to help you with your homework?
4 I'll help you with your project if you like.

3 **Group conversation**

Work in small groups. Half the group is in a difficult situation. Decide what this is.
Half the group writes offers of help. The other half prepares ways to respond.
Act out your conversation. Use the expressions in the boxes above.

Listening comprehension

1 **Look at the four pairs of pictures. Describe the people.**

2 🎧 **Listen to the people above talking. Circle where their conversations take place.**

1 a in the street   b in an airport   c at a railway station
2 a in the kitchen   b in the sitting room   c at a hospital
3 a in a bedroom   b in the sitting room   c in the kitchen
4 a in the street   b in the park   c at the beach

3 🎧 **Listen again and answer these questions.**
1 In number 1, what did the man do? Why?
2 In number 2, what do you think has happened to the boy? Who is the girl? Why is the boy annoyed with her?
3 In number 3, what is the woman cooking? Why? Who is the boy?
4 In number 4, what happened to the cyclist?
5 Which people accept help? Which people refuse help?

4 **Work in pairs. Choose one of the situations and act it out.**

Writing features

A travelogue

The article on Istanbul is a **personal account** of the writer's visits to the city. She has described it in detail; given some historical information about it; and written about what she **likes** and **dislikes** about it. She has not just researched it from books or the internet. She has actually been to Istanbul and experienced the city **first hand**.

Checklist
Look again at the article *Istanbul – a city of two continents* on pages 62 and 63.

▶	**Introduction**	There isn't much point in reading about a place if you don't know where in the world it is! The writer begins by explaining where Istanbul is, e.g. At the eastern end of Europe …
		Find two more phrases that tell you where Istanbul is.
▶	**First person**	This is a personal account and is written in the *first person*, e.g. I've always found it … To me …
		Find two more examples of the first person.
▶	**Second person**	The writer uses the *second person* to 'draw the reader in' and make them want to visit Istanbul, e.g. … will be just right for you …, … if you get the chance …
		Find two more examples of the second person.
▶	**Tenses**	The writer uses *present tenses* when writing about Istanbul as it is now, e.g. … there is a vast and fascinating city …
		She uses *past tenses* when writing about how it was, e.g. … armies besieged and captured the city …
		Find two more examples of present and past tenses.
▶	**Information / Facts**	*Information* in this type of writing can include historical and present day facts, e.g. historical: The city itself was established a thousand years earlier; present day: Land and houses are expensive …
		Find two more examples of historical and present day facts.
▶	**Personal opinion**	An important aspect of a personal account is that the writer expresses *opinions*. These can be positive opinions, e.g. I find it truly uplifting …
		These can be negative opinions, e.g. Traffic is one of my least favourite things …
		Find two more examples of positive and negative opinions that the writer expresses about the city.
▶	**Description**	The writer's opinion is also expressed through *descriptive* words and phrases, e.g. beautiful, magnificent, … horns blaring and smelling like old oil cans.
		Find two more examples of descriptive words and phrases that shows how the writer feels about Istanbul.

Writing assignment
You have read and discussed a personal account of the writer's visits to Istanbul.
You are now going to write your own personal account.
Choose a town or city you know well.
Write a personal account giving information, detailed description and expressing your opinion.

Go to p66 in your Workbook for help with your planning.

Writing features: a travelogue

Study skills 2

Research

> **What is research?**
> **Research** is making a detailed study of something for a particular purpose.

1 The first step is to know what you are researching and why. When you have done your research, what type of writing will you have to do?

- **A factual report**

To write a factual report, you need to research the facts and present the information in a clear, organised way.
Factual topics could include: Mount Everest: Reaching the top
The life of a famous sports person
The seven wonders of the ancient world

> **Activity**
>
> Think of more examples of topics that require a factual report.

- **A discursive essay**

To write a discursive essay, you need to research the facts and understand the different points of view.
Discursive topics could include:

Fast food is very popular and saves time for busy working people. However, many experts say that it is not completely healthy. What can you say for and against fast food?

Many people enjoy watching television. However, some people believe it can be harmful. What can you say for and against watching television?

> **Activity**
>
> Think of more examples of topics that require a discursive essay.

2 The next step is to read the question / title very carefully and underline the key words.

For example: *The life of a famous sports person*
[Not a musician or an actor!]

Fast food is very popular and saves time for busy working people. However, many experts say that it is not completely healthy. What can you say for and against fast food?
[Not do you like / dislike fast food!]

> **Activity**
>
> What key words would you underline in the other topics in Activity 1?

3 Make notes on any information / ideas you have about the topic first.

You may be surprised at how much you already know, e.g.
Mount Everest – highest mountain in the world

4 Write notes / questions on what you need to find out.

For example, *Where exactly is Mount Everest? How high is it? Who reached the top first?*

> **Activity**
>
> As a class, discuss the topic *Mount Everest: Reaching the top*. Make notes on what you already know, and what you need to find out.
> Do the same for the topic about watching television.

Sources

Sources are what you use to find information about your topic. The two main sources are printed material and the internet.

- **Printed material**

This includes books, newspapers and magazines. You can't be expected to read everything, so use contents pages and indexes to narrow down your search.

The contents page is at the beginning of a book and shows you chapter headings and page numbers.

> Contents
> Chapter 1: How mountains are made   6
> Chapter 2: The Andes   12
> Chapter 3: The Himalayas   25

An index is at the back of a book and has topics listed in alphabetical order with page numbers.

Make notes on anything you think will be useful.

> Index
> Andes   12–24
> Himalayas   25–36

Look back at Level 7, Unit 3 and Level 8, Unit 11 to remind yourself about note taking.

- **The internet**

There is an enormous amount of information on the internet and you shouldn't believe everything you read! Look carefully at the web address and decide whether you can 'trust' it. Ask your teacher for help if you are unsure.

You are researching the topic of cars and you find articles on the internet from these addresses:

> S. Downs *The History of the Motor Car*   http://www.motoring-history.com
> C. Clarke *Cars are fun*   http://www.fred.com

Which of these would you use? Why?

Bibliography

A bibliography comes at the end of your work. This is a list of the sources you have used. Keep a list of the printed material and the websites you have used as you go along.

Present them at the end of your work like this:

- printed material:

author / date published / title, e.g. Smith, P (2009) *Climbing Everest*

- internet sources:

author / date / title / web address, e.g.

Firth, K (2010) *Fast Food In Modern Life* http://www.healthyliving.com

Glossary

chapter: one of the sections of a book
index: an alphabetical list of subjects or names at the back of a book that shows on which page they are mentioned
source: a person, place or thing that provides something that you need

WB p120

It's a classic

Start-up Use WB p71 for your notes.

▶ Many famous classic novels, which are long pieces of fiction, were written more than a hundred years ago. Some were first published in magazines. Each week, a few chapters appeared. The complete book was published later.

▲ When a classic is made into a film for the cinema or TV, the story is told through dialogue and action. The script brings the narrative (descriptions of events) to life and audiences enjoy a thrilling plot.

▲ Classics are known for being the best writing. They may have several hundred pages. Many classics have been made shorter and simpler so they are easier to read. These are abridged versions.

What classic fiction do you know of in any language? List three titles.
What classics have you read in school?
Have you read abridged or original versions? Have you read any translations?
Why do you think you are encouraged to read classics?

Reading
- You will read an extract from a famous classic novel called *War and Peace*. Find out who wrote it, when and the nationality of the author.

Vocabulary
- These words are in the extract: dainty   swiftly   shyly   scurry. Circle any you cannot remember or guess. Look them up.
- Find out what these phrases mean: goodness gracious   darling   on the eve of the new year.

Grammar
- You will study sentences with **the indirect object as the subject of a passive sentence**. The classic extract is about a family. The family has been sent an invitation to a special event. Has your family ever been sent an invitation to a special event?

Word focus
- Dictionary: You will find out how a dictionary can help you **extend your vocabulary**. Think of at least five different words that mean 'big'.
- Spelling: You will look at plurals with *-s* / *-es*. Think of three words that have the plural *-es*.
- Suffix: The suffix *-ic* makes adjectives from nouns. What do you think *dramatic* means? What noun does it come from?

▶ Some of the most famous classics in English are by Shakespeare and Dickens. Their gripping plots and fascinating, colourful characters put them among the most popular writers in the language.

▲ Classic fiction is written in many languages and has settings in many different cultures. The best novels are translated into other languages so that more people can enjoy them.

▲▼ The settings of classic novels may seem strange to modern readers. Clothes and objects are mentioned that are no longer used. Often, readers have to understand new words and expressions.

Grammar in use
- You will hear a discussion about a problem that the festival committee must solve. Think of three things that could go wrong with the arrangements they have made so far.
- You will study **pronouns and possessive adjectives**. What does a pronoun replace? What information does a possessive adjective give you about a noun?

Listening and speaking
- You will listen to the festival committee's emergency meeting about the problem they face. If a group of people has to meet to discuss an emergency, what is it important for everyone to do during the meeting? Think of three things.
- You will prepare a presentation about your favourite author. Can you list six authors?

Conversation focus 🎧 2.05
At the end of an orchestra rehearsal, Giorgio, Gustav and Florence discuss classics.
1. Listen to their conversation about classic fiction. How many classic authors do they mention?
2. Read the questions on Workbook page 71. Listen again and answer the questions.
3. Talk in a group about classic fiction that you know of in any language. Use the photos and information on this page to help you, as well as any of your own ideas. Ask: *Have you read …? Have you seen …? Do you prefer …?* Say: *I have / haven't read …, I have / haven't heard of …, I've seen / watched …, I prefer …*

Writing
- You will write a narrative extract about a new experience. You can choose what the setting is. You will think of the character who experiences the new event and write about him or her. Will you write in the first or third person?

A New Year Ball

Seventeen-year-old Natasha Rostov is visiting St Petersburg with her parents, the Count and Countess Rostov, and her cousin, Sonya. The family has been sent an invitation to a special event. In this extract, the writer recounts Natasha's excitement and her wish that all the family should look their very best.

On the 31st December, on the eve of the new year of 1810, an old grandee of Catherine's day was giving a ball to see out the old year. The diplomatic corps and the Emperor were to be present.

The grandee's well-known mansion on the English Quay blazed with innumerable lights. Police were stationed at the brilliantly-lit, red-carpeted entrance – not only gendarmes but the chief of police himself and dozens of officers. Carriages drove away, and new ones kept arriving with red-liveried footmen and grooms in plumed hats. From the carriages emerged men wearing uniform, stars and ribbons, while ladies in satin and ermine cautiously descended the carriage steps which were let down for them with a clatter, and swiftly and noiselessly passed along the red baize into the porch.

… Already a third of the guests had arrived, but the Rostovs, who were to be present, were still hurrying to get dressed. …

Natasha was going to her first grand ball. She had got up at eight that morning and had been in a fever of excitement and energy all day. All her energies from the moment she woke had been directed to the one aim of ensuring that they all – herself, mama and Sonya – should look their very best. Sonya and the countess put themselves entirely in her hands. …

Sonya was nearly ready, so was the countess; but Natasha, who had bustled about helping everyone, was less advanced. She was still sitting before the looking-glass with a peignoir thrown over her thin shoulders. Sonya, on the last stage, stood in the middle of the room fastening on a final bow and hurting her dainty finger as she pressed the pin that squeaked as it went through the ribbon.

"Not like that, Sonya, not like that!" cried Natasha, turning her head and clutching with both hands at her hair which the maid, who was dressing it, had not time to let go. "That bow isn't right. Come here!"

Sonya sat down and Natasha pinned the ribbon differently.

"If you please, miss, I can't get on like this," said the maid, still holding Natasha's hair.

"Oh, goodness gracious, wait then! There, that's better, Sonya."

"Will you soon be ready?" came the countess's voice. "It is nearly ten."

"Coming, coming! What about you, mama?"

"I have only my cap to pin on."

"Don't do it without me!" cried Natasha. "You won't do it right."

"Yes, but it's ten o'clock."

It had been agreed they should arrive at the ball at half past ten, but Natasha had still to get her dress on before they called for Madam Peronsky.

When her hair was done, Natasha, in a short petticoat from under which her dancing-slippers showed, and her mother's dressing-jacket, ran up to Sonya, inspected her critically, and then flew on to her mother. Turning the countess's head this way and that, she fastened on the cap, gave the grey hair a hasty kiss and scurried back to the maids who were shortening her skirt.

The cause of the delay was Natasha's skirt, which was too long. Two maids were at work turning up the hem and hurriedly biting off the threads. A third, with her mouth full of pins, was running backwards and forwards between the countess and Sonya, while a fourth held the gossamer garment high on one uplifted hand.

"Hurry up, Mavra, darling!"

"Hand me that thimble, please, miss."

"Aren't you ever going to be ready?" asked the count, coming to the door. "Here you are, still perfuming yourselves. Madam Peronsky must be tired of waiting."

"Ready, miss," said the maid, lifting up the shortened tulle skirt with two fingers … Natasha began putting on the dress.

"In a minute, in a minute! Don't come in, papa!" she cried to her father at the door, her face eclipsed in a cloud of tulle. Sonya slammed the door to. But a moment later they let the count in. He was wearing a blue swallow-tail coat, stockings and buckled shoes, and was perfumed and pomaded.

"Oh, papa, how nice you look! Lovely!" exclaimed Natasha, as she stood in the middle of the room, stroking out the folds of her tulle.

"If you please, miss, allow me," said the maid, who was on her knees pulling the skirt straight, and shifting the pins from one side of her mouth to the other with her tongue.

"You can say what you like," cried Sonya in despairing tones, as she surveyed Natasha's dress, "You can say what you like, it is still too long!"

Natasha stepped back to see herself in the pier-glass. The dress was too long.

"Really, madam, it is not at all too long," said Mavra, crawling on her knees after her young lady.

"Well, if it's too long we'll tack it up … we can do it in a second," said the determined Dunyasha …

At that moment the countess in her cap and velvet gown crept shyly into the room.

"Oo-oo, my beauty!" cried the count. "She looks nicer than any of you!"

He would have embraced her but blushing, she stepped back, for fear of getting her gown rumpled.

"Mama, your cap wants to go more to one side," said Natasha. "I'll alter it for you," and she darted forward so that the maids who were tacking up her skirt could not follow her fast enough and a piece of the tulle got torn off.

"Mercy, what was that? Really it was not my fault …"

"Never mind, I'll put a stitch in it, it won't show," said Dunyasha.

"My beauty – my little queen!" exclaimed the old nurse, coming in at the door. "And little Sonya, too! Ah, the beauties! …"

At last at a quarter past ten they seated themselves in the carriage and were on their way.

From *War and Peace* by Leo Tolstoy

Glossary

grandee:	an older person who has done important work in government
diplomatic corps:	the group of people who represent the governments of other countries
English Quay:	an elegant street in St Petersburg
gendarme:	a policeman
a dozen:	a group of twelve of something
peignoir:	a thin robe like a dressing gown
thimble:	a metal cover that fits on a finger to protect it when sewing
swallow-tail coat:	an old-fashioned kind of coat
pomaded:	with hair dressed in oil or ointment
pier-glass:	a tall mirror for looking at the whole body
nurse:	a servant who looks after the young children of a rich family

Note: Catherine – Catherine the Great, Empress of Russia 1762–1796

Reading comprehension

1 Write the name of the person next to the words they said.
Write *Natasha*, *Countess*, *Count*, *Sonya*, *Dunyasha* or *Nurse*.

1. That bow isn't right. Come here! ....
2. I have only my cap to pin on. ....
3. Don't do it without me! ....
4. Will you soon be ready? ....
5. Oh, goodness gracious, wait then! ....
6. … you can say what you like, it is still too long! ....
7. Aren't you ever going to be ready? ....
8. Hurry up, Mavra, darling! ....
9. She looks nicer than any of you. ....
10. In a minute, in a minute! ....
11. … how nice you look! Lovely! ....
12. Well, if it's too long we'll tack it up … ....
13. Really it was not my fault … ....
14. My beauty – my little queen! ....

2 Discuss these questions about the characters.

1. Look at the lines in Activity 1.
   a. Which character said most of the lines in Activity 1?
   b. Which character uses the imperative form of the verb most often? How many times?
   c. Which characters ask questions?
   d. Which character's speech is punctuated with the most exclamation marks?
2. Discuss what Natasha says and does in the extract. How would you describe her character?
3. Is Sonya different to Natasha? How does she behave? Describe her character.
4. Do you think Natasha has a good relationship with her mother and father? How can you tell? Find evidence in the text.

3 Match the phrases on the left to the meanings on the right.

1. entirely in someone's hands ....   a. go down carefully
2. cautiously descend ....   b. look at carefully
3. creep shyly ....   c. intention to make certain
4. aim of ensuring ....   d. completely under someone's control
5. inspect critically ....   e. walk quietly not wanting to be noticed

4 Discuss your answers to these questions.

1. Why do you think Natasha is so excited about this ball?
2. Why do you think the countess and Sonya put themselves 'entirely in the hands' of Natasha while they are getting ready?
3. Do you think the Rostov's often go to a grand ball like this? Find evidence for your answer.
4. Do you think Natasha is going to enjoy this ball? Why? / Why not?

5 What do you think?

- Would you enjoy going to a grand ball? Why? / Why not?
- How would you feel when you were getting ready for the ball?
- If you were going to a ball with your family, would you prefer someone like Natasha or someone like Sonya as part of your family group? Why?

Grammar

1 Read.

At last it was the evening of the ball! **The family had been sent an invitation** weeks before and ever since, Natasha had been counting the days, wishing for this moment to arrive. She had spent the day making sure that all the family looked their very best and now she was in a hurry to get dressed herself. **Natasha had been bought a new dress by her father** but it was too long. There was no time to lose. One maid held up the dress. Two more pinned up the hem. **The fourth maid was handed a thimble** and quickly set to work with her needle and thread.

Some time later the Rostov's carriage arrived at a mansion on the English Quay. In a blaze of lights, **the family** descended the carriage steps and **were shown the way by servants in red and gold uniforms** along the red carpet and into the ballroom ...

2 Answer these questions.
1. What had the Rostovs been sent?
2. How had Natasha spent the day?
3. What had she been bought by her father?
4. What was the problem with the dress?
5. Where was the ball held?
6. How did the family find the ballroom?

3 Underline the indirect objects in these active sentences. The first one has been done for you.
1. Her father had bought <u>Natasha</u> a new dress.
2. Someone handed a thimble to the maid.
3. Servants showed the family the way to the ballroom.
4. Someone has given Jenny a bouquet of flowers.
5. Someone must teach French to the boys.
6. Professor Martin will show the students a film.

4 Now make the sentences in Activity 3 passive. In each sentence the indirect object will become the subject. Use a *by* phrase where necessary.

1. *Natasha had been bought a new dress by her father.*

5 Make more passive sentences as in the example.
1. yesterday – I – send – strange email
   Yesterday I was sent a strange email.
2. last week – our class – set – a difficult test
3. next month – some students – award – prizes for their work
4. the boy – lend – camera – his father
5. we – tell – an interesting story – our teacher
6. the guests – bring – food and drink – smartly-dressed servants

6 Answer these questions. Talk about your answers in small groups.
1. Have you ever been given a special present? What was it? Who gave it to you?
2. Have you ever been sent an invitation? What was the occasion? Did you go?
3. Have you ever been told a funny story? Who told it to you? Can you retell it?

The indirect object as the subject of a passive sentence

When you change an active sentence into a passive sentence, the object becomes the subject:
*Someone stole **our car**.* →
***Our car** was stolen.*
The **indirect object** of an active sentence can also become the subject.
*Someone sent an email to **him**.* →
***He** was sent an email.*
*Her wealthy uncle gave **her** a present.* →
***She** was given a present by her wealthy uncle.*

Word focus

A Dictionary work Build Your Vocabulary boxes

Build Your Vocabulary boxes bring together words that are related to a particular subject or suggest other words you can use instead of very common ones.

| cause | /kɔːz/ | verb | [T] | to make something happen, usually something bad: *Bad weather continues to **cause** problems for travellers.* |

> Build Your Vocabulary: words you can use instead of **cause**.
> - **bring about** to make something happen, especially something positive that improves the situation
> - **give rise to** to make something happen, especially something unpleasant or unexpected
> - **lead to** to begin a process that makes something happen later
> - **contribute to** to be one of several causes that help to make something happen

Complete these sentences by using the best phrase from the Build Your Vocabulary box above.
1. Driving cars .... global warming.
2. This plan will .... a great improvement.
3. These ideas will .... a successful festival.
4. This heavy rain will .... flooding.

B Spelling Revision: plurals with -s and -es

> Most nouns make their plural by adding -s, e.g.
> light → lights   star → stars

1 Reread *A New Year Ball* and find five more examples of plural nouns with **-s**.

> Nouns ending in -ss, -ch, -sh and -x make their plural by adding -es, e.g.
> dress → dresses   stitch → stitches

2 Make these nouns plural by adding **-s** or **-es**.

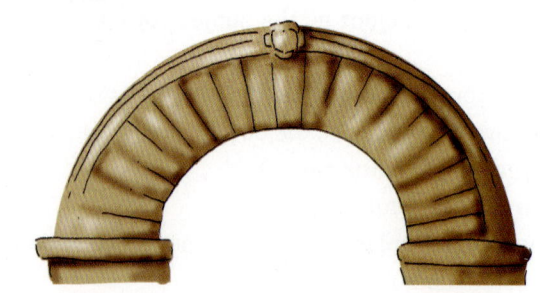

1 box   2 guest   3 arch
4 finger   5 bush   6 torch
7 shoe   8 bunch   9 glass

C Word groups Things people wear

From the extract:
1. Find two things people **wear on their head**.
2. Find three things people wear **beginning with s**.
3. Find three more things people wear.

D Suffixes -ic

> Adding the suffix **-ic** can change a noun into an adjective, e.g.
> diplomat → diplomatic
> *The **diplomatic** corps and the Emperor were to be present.*

1 Add the suffix **-ic** to these nouns to make adjectives. Use your dictionary to check spelling.

1 athlete   2 acid   3 hero
4 majesty   5 poet   6 artist

2 Complete these sentences with **-ic** adjectives. Use the noun in brackets.

1. There are many .... buildings in Istanbul. (history)
2. He lead a .... life, moving from place to place. (nomad)
3. .... ash covered the town after the eruption. (volcano)
4. The laboratory was full of .... instruments. (science)

Grammar in use

1 🔊 **Listen and read.**

Miss Jackson: Ramon Acosta! Stop! **You** know running is forbidden in school.
Ramon: Sorry, Miss Jackson.
Miss Jackson: Where are **you** going so fast?
Ramon: **I**'m looking for Todd. **I**'ve got to find **him**. There's been a disaster.
Miss Jackson: Oh, dear! What's happened?
Ramon: Eliza Brodie, the author, has cancelled. **She** can't come to the festival. I've just had an email from **her**.
Miss Jackson: That is bad news. Did **she** give a reason?
Ramon: "Personal problems".
Miss Jackson: Hmm ... That's disappointing. Isn't there anyone else **we** can ask?
Ramon: **I** don't know. **It**'s such short notice. And **her** name's on the posters. And what about the tickets? **We**'ve sold loads of **them**!
Miss Jackson: Calm down, Ramon! Don't panic! That won't get **us** anywhere.
Ramon: But **I** don't know what to do!
Miss Jackson: Leave **it** with **me** for the moment. **I**'m going to make a phone call. Perhaps a friend of **mine** can help.
Ramon: Really?
Miss Jackson: Well, **it**'s a long shot but **you** never know. Go and explain the situation to the committee. I saw **them** in the library. And Ramon ...
Ramon: Yes, Miss Jackson?
Miss Jackson: Don't run!

2 Answer these questions.
1. Why is Ramon running?
2. What disaster has happened?
3. Why is this a problem?
4. Can Miss Jackson definitely help?
5. What is she going to do?

3 Change the sentences as in the example.
1. Please, pass the dictionary to me.
   Please, pass me the dictionary.
2. I sent an email to him.
3. Uncle Jim brought presents for us.
4. I made a cake for them.
5. He bought a dress for her.
6. I'll show my photos to you.

4 Ask and answer in pairs.
1. your book?
   A: Is this your book? B: Yes, it's mine.
2. Miss Jackson's car?
3. our results?
4. my essay?
5. the students' idea?
6. Gustav's violin?

5 Change the sentences to include noun + *of* + possessive pronoun.
1. James is one of my friends.
   James is a friend of mine.
2. Amanda is one of our cousins.
3. I've read one of her books.
4. Is music one of your hobbies?
5. Impatience is one of his faults.
6. This mansion is just one of their houses.

> **Subject pronouns:** *I, you, he, she, it, we, they*
> **I** am tired. **He** is clever. **They** are students.
> **Direct object pronouns:** *me, you, him, her, it, us, them*
> We can see **him**. Can he see **us**?
> **Indirect object pronouns:** *me, you, him, her, it, us, them*
> Please lend your book to **me**. Please lend **me** your book.
> **Possessive pronouns:** *mine, yours, his, hers, ours, theirs*
> Is this book **yours**? Jenny is a friend of **mine**.
> **Possessive adjectives:** *my, your, his, her, its, our, their*
> I love **my** town and **its** noisy, crowded streets.

Look at the dialogue in Activity 1 above and find examples of pronouns (subject, direct object, indirect object and possessive). Also find examples of possessive adjectives.

Grammar in use: pronouns (subject, direct object, indirect object, possessive); possessive adjectives

Listening and speaking

Listening comprehension

1. 🎧 **The students on the festival committee are talking in the library. Listen and answer these questions.**
   1. What is the problem?
   2. Who has solved the problem? How?
   3. How do the students feel?

2. 🎧 **Listen again and write T (true), F (false) or NS (not stated). Correct the false statements.**
   1. At the beginning of the conversation Ramon is perfectly calm.
   2. Miss Jackson spent half an hour on the phone.
   3. Anthony Holt was delighted to hear from Miss Jackson.
   4. Anthony Holt is a well-known writer of science fiction.
   5. The students are not sure if they want him to appear at the festival.
   6. Anthony Holt is an old friend of Miss Jackson's.
   7. They studied the same subject at university.
   8. Anthony Holt is in America writing a new book.
   9. Anthony Holt wants *Black Star* to be turned into a film.
   10. The students are going to send him a letter.
   11. Todd will make an announcement on the website.
   12. Todd suggests putting stickers on the posters.

3. **Talk about the statements which you marked NS (not stated). Why did you choose these answers?**

4. **Talk about it.**
   If you went to the festival, would you be interested in listening to Anthony Holt's talk? Why? / Why not?

Individual speaking

You are going to talk about your favourite author.
Preparation in groups:
1. Find out which authors the group likes best. Make a list.
2. What type of books do these authors write?
3. Which books of theirs do you know? Write down three titles.
4. What are these books about? Describe one of the plots.
5. Have any of these books been made into films or TV programmes? If so, did you like them? Why? / Why not?

Now tell the rest of the class about your discussion. *WB p77*

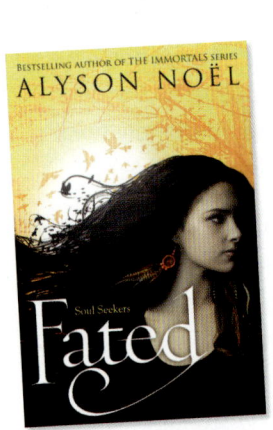

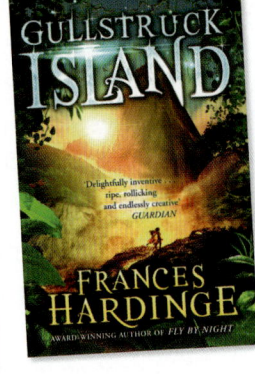

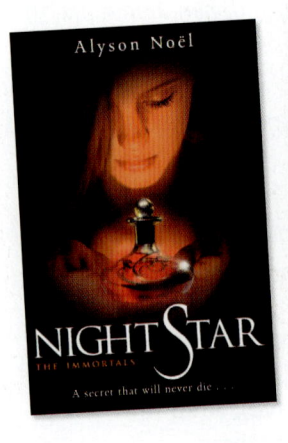

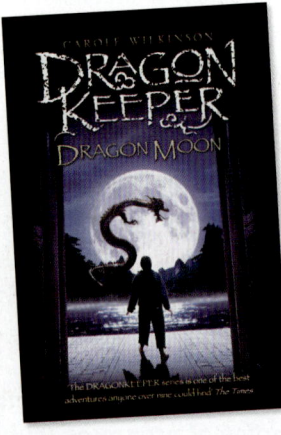

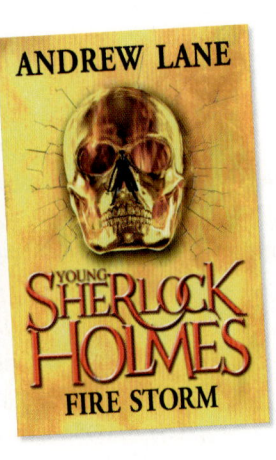

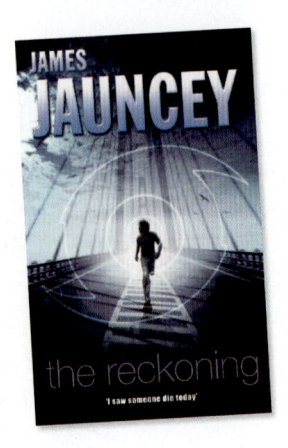

Writing features

Narrative extract

> The narrative extract you have read from *War and Peace* concentrates on the character of Natasha and her preparations for 'her first grand ball'.
>
> Readers can tell how Natasha is feeling about the situation through her speech and actions.

Checklist

Look again at the extract *A New Year Ball* on pages 74 and 75.

▶ **Common features of narrative writing**

Throughout the course, you have studied examples of narrative writing and you know they have the following *features* in common: setting, character, plot and past tenses.

In class or groups, discuss and make notes on the following:
- the setting

What are the three settings in the extract?
- the characters

Which characters do we only know by name? Who are the main characters?
- the plot

What happens in each of the three settings? Find examples of past tenses in the extract.

▶ **Description**

In the extract, the author has used *description*:
- to set the scene at the ball at the mansion, e.g. blazed with innumerable lights.
- for the characters' clothes, e.g. red-liveried footmen, a blue swallow-tail coat.

Find other examples of the description of the mansion and the clothes.

▶ **Characters' feelings**

After a description of the mansion where the ball is to be held, the scene moves to the Rostov's house and centres on Natasha. The author wants readers to understand how Natasha is feeling about her 'first grand ball'. He does this through:

- what Natasha does, e.g. She had got up at eight that morning … a fever of excitement and energy all day …
- using strong verbs to describe her actions, e.g. bustled, clutching, ran.
- what Natasha says, e.g. Don't do it without me … You won't do it right.
- using synonyms for *said*, e.g. cried, exclaimed.

We know that Natasha is excited about the ball. All her energies from the moment she woke had been directed to the one aim of ensuring that they all – herself, her mother and Sonya – should look their very best.

Find examples of what Natasha does and says that show her excitement and her determination that everyone should look their best.

Examine how:
- Natasha gets involved with how her mother and Sonya are dressed.
- difficult Natasha makes the maids' job of helping her to get ready.

Look for strong verbs.

Writing assignment

You have read and discussed *A New Year Ball*, which shows how one character is feeling about something that is going to happen. You are now going to write your own narrative extract about a character preparing for a new experience.

It is a good idea to write from your own experience, e.g. preparing for the first day at a new school / first time on an aeroplane / first time in a school sports team.

Go to p78 in your Workbook for help with your planning.

Finding out

Start-up *Use WB p81 for your notes.*

▶ Electricity occurs naturally but people did not discover how to create it and control it until 200 years ago. This energy source is crucial to modern industry, supplying transport, heating, lighting and computing.

▼ We use modern inventions every day. We are so used to the benefits they bring to our lives that we rarely give any thought to how they work.

▲ A fully loaded, fuelled plane carrying about 400 passengers weighs more than 300,000 kilograms. That is about the weight of a herd of 60 elephants. The plane accelerates along the runway, takes off into the air and stays up in the air until it lands again.

Which things mentioned on this page have you experienced?
Do you ever think about how they work? Why? / Why not?
What sort of things are you interested in finding out about?
What things do you need to find out about for your school work?

Reading
- You will read an article about human achievement in space flight and an explanation of how a space launch works. **About how many people do you think have flown in space?**

Vocabulary
- These words are in the article:
  achievement   satellite   orbit   mission   horizontal   altitude. Circle any you cannot remember or guess. Look them up.
- Find out what these phrases mean: *chemical reaction   maximum thrust.*

Grammar
- You will study the **future perfect simple passive**. **What homework subjects will have been given to you by the end of today?**

Word focus
- Dictionary: You will learn about **subject labels** in dictionary entries. **Think of three different school subjects that use special vocabulary.**
- Spelling: You will look at the plurals of words ending *-y*. **Think of a word ending *-ey* and one ending consonant + *-y*.**
- Prefixes: You will look at words beginning with the prefix **re-**. **In *reread*, what do you think *re-* means?**

8

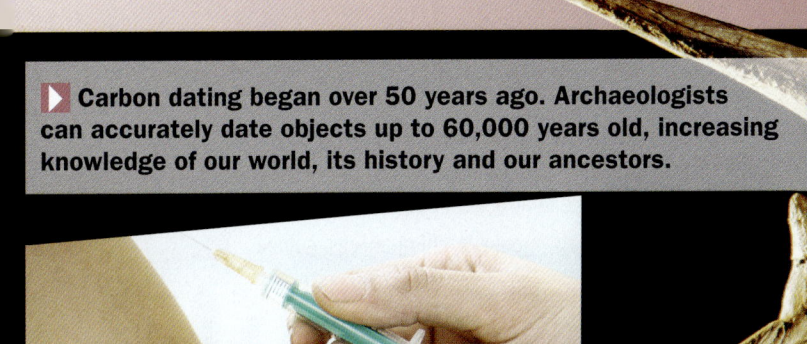

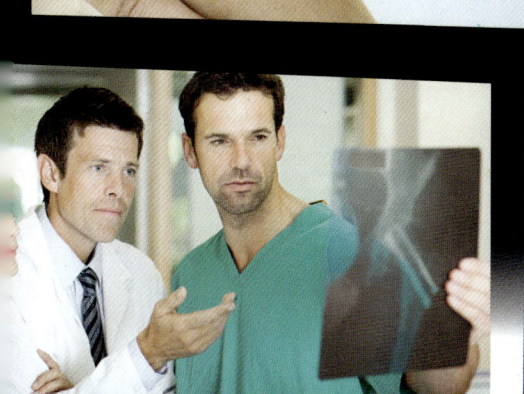

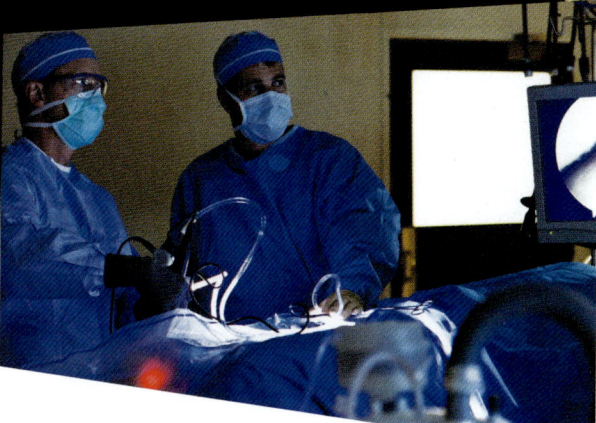

▶ Carbon dating began over 50 years ago. Archaeologists can accurately date objects up to 60,000 years old, increasing knowledge of our world, its history and our ancestors.

◀ Doctors have been preventing diseases by giving vaccinations for more than 200 years. They examine injuries by X-ray and perform keyhole surgery using fibre optic cameras and lasers.

Grammar in use
- You will hear a discussion about final arrangements for the festival.
  Think of five events that the committee has arranged for the festival.
- You will study **separable** and **inseparable phrasal verbs**.
  What does *separable* mean? What does *inseparable* mean?

Listening and speaking
- You will learn and practise expressions for making requests and giving or refusing permission politely. Which is the most important word to add to a request to make it polite?
- You will listen to a conversation in which a person arrives after a terrible journey.
  Think of three things that could make a journey terrible.

Conversation focus 🎧 2.09
Kurt is using the library computer, which has a catalogue of all the books.
1. Listen to his conversation with Mimi and Florence about finding out about how things work.
2. Read the questions on Workbook page 81. Listen again and answer the questions.
3. Talk in a group about things you are interested in finding out about. Use the photos to help you, as well as any of your own ideas. Ask: *What do you need to find out about …? Why? Do you know …? Are you more interested in …?* Say: *I'd like to find out about … because …, I know how …, I'm more interested in finding out …*

Writing
- You will write an explanation of how something happens now or how something used to happen. Which tenses do you think you would use for each of these explanations?

▲ Every day, people use computers, mobile phones, email and the internet to communicate around the world 24/7.

83

Human achievement – spaceflight

Spaceflight testing

The first living creatures in space were flies. They were sent by the USA to the edge of space in a rocket in 1947 and were recovered alive. A succession of test flights involving animals came after, including dogs, cats, monkeys, chimpanzees, guinea pigs, frogs, tortoises, rats and various fish. Unfortunately, not all came back alive.

First human spaceflights

Russian cosmonaut Yuri Gagarin was the first man in space and he orbited Earth on 12th April, 1961. The first woman in space was Russian cosmonaut Valentina Tereshkova on 16th June, 1963. The first man on the moon was USA astronaut Neil Armstrong, in 1969.

Spaceflight development

Following the first flights, different space transportation systems were developed using rocket engines. One system, the US Shuttle program, ran from 1981–2011 and flew 135 missions during which satellites and probes were launched.

The Magellan probe sent back pictures of Venus.

The International Space Station is an artificial satellite that people can live on.

How does a rocket engine work?

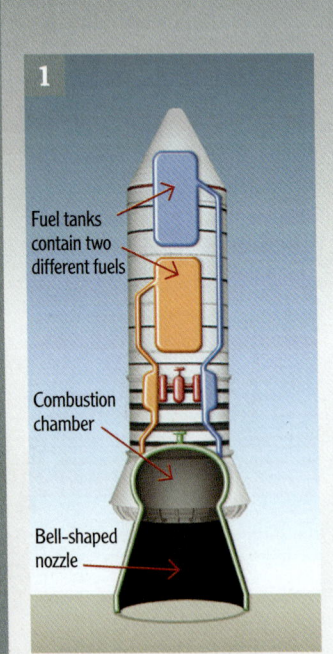

If you blow a balloon full of air (gas) then immediately let it go, the balloon will fly away from you as the gas spurts out of the opening at a very fast rate.

A rocket engine for launching into space works in the same way but on a much bigger scale and uses fuel to make gas.

1 Fuel tanks contain two different fuels / Combustion chamber / Bell-shaped nozzle

First, the fuels are combined in the combustion chamber.

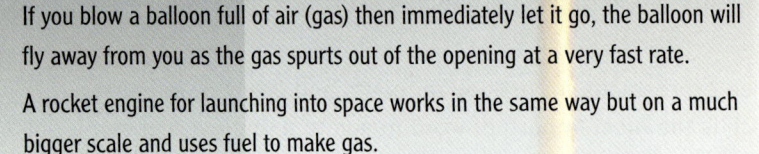

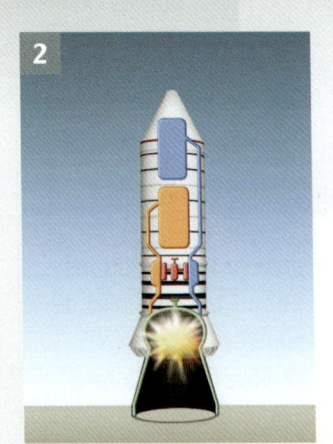

2 *A chemical reaction creates a controlled explosion.*

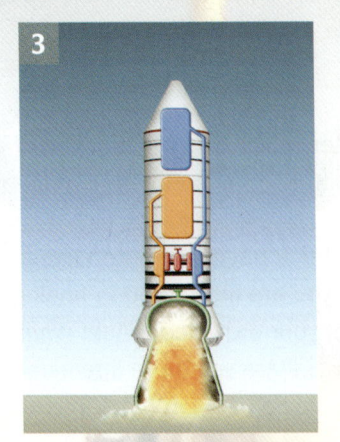

3 *The explosion produces burning gas, which is forced out of the nozzle at very high speed.*

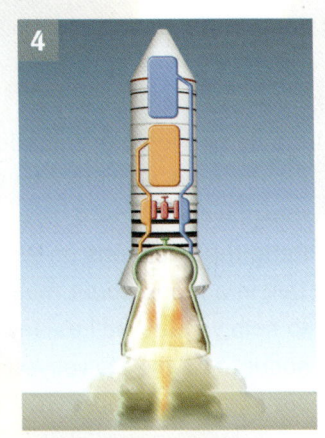

4 *The energy created by the burning gas pushes the rocket upwards.*

How was the shuttle launched?

The shuttle 'stack' was made up of two Solid Rocket Boosters (SRBs), the External Tank (ET) and the orbital spacecraft. The SRBs helped the shuttle to lift off. The ET contained the fuel needed to launch into space. Fully fuelled, the shuttle stack weighed six million kilograms, so it needed a lot of energy to take off. The orbital spacecraft had three main engines. These engines, combined with the SRBs, created sufficient energy to lift the shuttle off the ground and into orbit through a sequence of controlled stages.

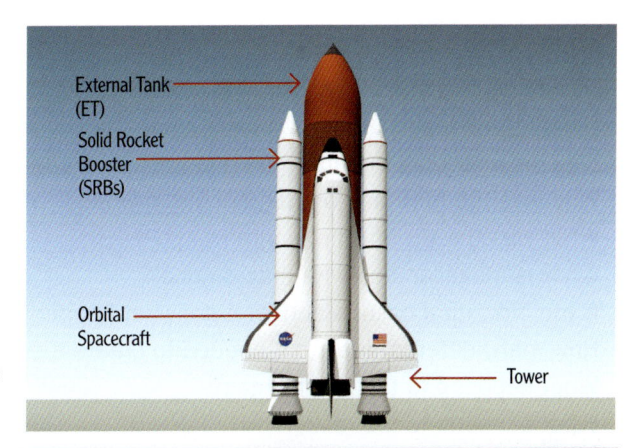

At the start of the launch sequence, 30 seconds before lift-off, the spacecraft's computers took over control. Six seconds before lift-off, the shuttle's main engines ignited one at a time, 0.12 seconds apart, and built up to more than 90 per cent of their maximum thrust. Three seconds before lift-off, the main engines were in lift-off position.

At the moment of lift-off, the SRBs were ignited. From this point, the launch was irreversible. The supports that held the stack to the tower were broken and the shuttle lifted up and off the launch pad. As the shuttle rose it turned slowly to the right and gradually took a more horizontal flight path. After one minute, the shuttle engines were at maximum thrust in order to maintain the lift-off.

After two minutes of flight, the SRBs had lifted the shuttle to an altitude of 45 kilometres. They then separated from the orbiter and fuel tank. Parachutes opened out from the SRBs and they fell to the ocean about 140 kilometres off the coast of Florida. They were recovered by the US Navy so that they could be reused for the next shuttle launch.

In the final launch stage, the main engines slowed down in order to stop the shuttle from going too fast and breaking up. After slowing down, they were shut down. The ET then separated from the orbiter and re-entered the Earth's atmosphere, burning up on re-entry. The orbiter's engines then fired up to take the spacecraft into low orbit around the Earth and carry out its mission.

Future spaceflights

Many nations are involved in space exploration and astronauts from 15 different countries have visited the ISS. Every year rockets are launched from sites around the world undertaking experiments, researching, and carrying probes and satellites into space. By the middle of this century, thousands of new space missions will have been completed. We can only guess at what they will have achieved.

Reading comprehension

1 **Discuss these questions.**
   1 When was the first rocket sent to the edge of space?
   2 Did all the animals sent into space come back alive?
   3 Which country did the first man and woman in space come from?
   4 Who was the first man on the moon and when?
   5 What was the US Shuttle program?
   6 What is Magellan and what has it done?
   7 If you blow up a balloon and let it go, what happens?
   8 How many different fuels are needed to create a controlled explosion?
   9 What happens to the burning gas?
   10 What happens to the rocket?

2 **Number these statements about the shuttle launch sequence in order.**
   a The main engines slowed down then shut down. ....
   b The orbiter's engines took it into low orbit. ....
   c The ET separated from the orbiter. ....
   d The main engines were in lift-off position. ....
   e The SRBs separated from the orbiter at an altitude of 45 kms. ....
   f The ET burned up on re-entry. ....
   g The shuttle's main engines ignited one at a time. ....
   h At lift off, the SRBs were ignited. ....
   i The spacecraft's computers took over control. ___1___
   j As the shuttle rose, it turned slowly to the right. ....

3 **Discuss your answers to these questions.**
   1 Why do you think animals were sent on test flights into space before humans?
   2 What things do you think were being tested?
   3 From the information in the text, what do you think is the benefit of a space station that is international?

4 **Discuss these issues in your groups.**
   1 a What do you think about animals being sent into space?
      b What do you think about people going into space?
      c Is there a difference between the two? What?
   2 Do you think spaceflight is a great achievement? Why? / Why not?

5 **What do you think?**
   - Imagine you are in orbit round the Earth in a spacecraft. You can see planet Earth below you.
     How would you feel and what would you think about?
   - Would you prefer a spacecraft flight to outer space or a plane flight to a destination of your choice?
     Give reasons for your preference.
   - Do you admire astronauts? Why? / Why not?

Grammar

1 Read.

In 1961 the first man went into space and orbited the Earth. During the years since then enormous advances have been made in the exploration of space. In 1969 the first men walked on the moon. Until 2011 the US Shuttle launched into space satellites, probes and telescopes, which have sent back spectacular photos of planets and stars. On the International Space Station (ISS) astronauts from many different countries conduct experiments and carry out research.

What about the future? We can safely say that by the middle of this century, thousands of new space missions **will have been completed**. What **will have been achieved** by these space flights? Thousands of experiments **will have been carried out** by scientists and thousands of pictures **will have been sent back** to Earth. By the year 2050 what fascinating discoveries **will have been made**? We can only guess.

2 Answer these questions.

1. When did the first men walk on the moon?
2. What did the US Shuttle do?
3. What happens on the ISS?
4. How many space missions will have been completed by the year 2050?
5. What will have been carried out by scientists in space?
6. Do we know what discoveries will have been made by the middle of this century?

3 Complete the sentences with the verbs from the box. Use the future perfect passive.

    increase   learn   discover   send
           make   carry out

1. By the end of the mission many important experiments ....
2. By the year 2050 thousands of new planets ....
3. By the middle of the century many new discoveries ....
4. Our understanding of the universe ....
5. Many new fascinating facts ....
6. Many new pictures .... back to Earth.

4 Use your own ideas to complete these sentences. Use the future perfect passive.

1. By the end of the week another rocket ...
2. By the end of the year a film about the ISS ...
3. When the astronauts return to Earth, 1,000 space missions ...

5 Work in pairs to make sentences using the future perfect passive.

1. Think about your school. What will have been achieved by the end of the year? Write three sentences.
2. Think about your town. What will have been achieved by the end of the decade? Write three sentences.

Compare your sentences with the rest of the class.

> We use the **future perfect passive** (*will + have been + past participle*):
> - when we are thinking about an action which will be completed before another action or a time in the future.
>
> By the end of the century many rockets **will have been launched**.
> By the time we arrive at the party, all the food **will have been eaten**.
>
> - when we are thinking about a continuous action before a time or event in the future.
>
> In July children **will have been taught** at this school for 50 years.
> When the old hospital is pulled down next year, it **will have been used** as a place to treat the sick for 500 years.
>
> If we want to stress who or what performs the action, we use *by* + noun.
>
> Many discoveries **will have been made by** the scientists on the Space Station.

Grammar: future perfect passive

Word focus

A Dictionary work Subject labels

Subject labels show whether a word belongs to a specialised subject.

astronaut   /ˈæstrəˌnɔːt/   noun [C]   ASTRONOMY someone who travels in space

1 Read these words from the passage.

rocket   flight   satellite   station   launch   moon

2 List the words you think belong to the specialised subject of astronomy.

3 Check in your dictionary. Were you correct?

B Spelling Revision: plurals of words ending in -y

If a word ends in vowel + -y, just add -s, e.g.
  monkey → monkeys
If a word ends in consonant + -y, change the y to i and add -es, e.g.
  fly → flies

Follow the rules and write the plurals of these words.

1 luxury   2 valley
3 duty   4 ability
5 highway   6 journey
7 industry   8 key
9 country   10 family
11 survey   12 century

C Word groups specialised subjects

1 Read these words from the article.

engine   gas   fuel   thrust
energy   atmosphere   experiment

2 Write the headings:

physics   science

3 Use your dictionary to a) check the meaning of each word in Activity 1 and b) find out to which specialised subject it belongs.

4 Write each word under the correct heading.

5 Which word have you written under both headings?

D Prefixes re-

The prefix re- can be put in front of almost any verb. It means again / once more, e.g.
  … they could be reused for the next shuttle launch.
A hyphen is normally used when the verb begins with e, e.g.
  The ET separated from the orbiter and re-entered the Earth's atmosphere.

1 Add the prefix re- to each of these verbs so that the action is done again.

1 appear   2 build
3 heat   4 think
5 arrange   6 read

2 Add the prefix re- to each of these verbs so that the action is done again. Some of these will need a hyphen.

1 encounter   2 enter
3 join   4 name
5 edit   6 elect

3 Use two re- words from Activity 1 and two re- words from Activity 2 in sentences of your own.

Grammar in use

Important!
Committee meeting
Library, 12.30 on the dot!
Don't be late!

1 🎧 2.11 Listen and read.

Todd: OK, let's **get on with** the meeting. We need to check all the last-minute details. For example, have we got enough helpers?
Tasha: More than enough. Loads of people **filled in** the forms.
Todd: Great. What about refreshments? Lucie, that's you.
Lucie: Everything's under control. The school canteen is providing drinks and Zafira's family **is bringing over** masses of delicious Lebanese snacks from their restaurant.
Todd: Brilliant.
Ramon: What about first aid, Todd? Suppose someone has an accident?
Todd: Miss Jones and Mr Day from the Science Department are qualified first-aiders. They're **helping** us **out**.
Tasha: I've been wondering about the end of the festival. Don't we need something spectacular to **finish** it **off**?
Todd: Lee, that new Chinese student, said he could probably **sort** something **out**. I'll let you know what he **comes up with**.
Ramon: Here's Rudi. Late as usual.
Rudi: Disaster! Disaster!
Lucie: Rudi! Whatever's the matter?
Rudi: It's the sculptures! They were outside in the garden and they've all disappeared!
Ramon: What? They can't have been stolen surely?
Tasha: Yes, maybe thieves have **made off with** them.
Todd: Well, if that's happened, it is a disaster ...

2 Cover the dialogue and read the statements. Write *True* or *False*. Correct the false statements.

1 They need more helpers. ....
2 Drinks will be provided by a Lebanese restaurant. ....
3 Two teachers can provide first aid if necessary. ....
4 How to end the festival is still undecided. ....
5 Rudi is in a panic. ....
6 The sculptures have definitely been stolen. ....

3 These sentences contain inseparable phrasal verbs. Change the sentences as in the example.

1 He got on his horse.
   He got on it.
2 They got on with their work.
3 They couldn't keep up with the boy.
4 My grandmother looked after my brother and me.
5 John fell out with his sister.
6 I came by these old photos at a market.

4 These sentences contain separable phrasal verbs. Change the sentences as in the example.

1 He chopped up the meat.
   He chopped the meat up. He chopped it up.
2 He gave back my book.
3 They handed over the keys.
4 He let down my sister and me.
5 He phoned up his aunt.
6 The scientists carried out experiments.

Phrasal verbs are **separable** or **inseparable**.
With **separable phrasal verbs** we can separate the verb and the preposition with the object or object pronoun.
*The student **filled in** the form.*
*The student **filled** the form **in**.*
*The student **filled** it **in**.*
With **inseparable phrasal verbs** we cannot separate the verb and the preposition with the object or object pronoun.
*She **looked after** the children.*
*She **looked after** them.*

Look at the phrasal verbs in the dialogue in Activity 1 above. Say if the phrasal verbs are separable or inseparable.

Grammar in use: separable and inseparable phrasal verbs

Listening and speaking

Functions of English: making requests
Asking someone to do something for you

1 Look at these useful expressions.

Can you ..., please? Could you ..., please?	Yes, of course. No problem.
Will you ..., please? Would you ..., please?	Sorry. I'm afraid not. I'm afraid I can't. Sorry.
Could you possibly ..., please?	

	No, not at all. Of course not.
Would you mind ... + gerund?	I can't, I'm afraid. Sorry.

Work in pairs. Using the expressions above, make requests and respond.
Ask your partner to ...

1 open the window.
2 lend you his/her dictionary.
3 help you with your homework.
4 test you on some irregular verbs.
5 check the spelling of some tricky words.

Asking for permission to do something

2 Look at these useful expressions.

Can I ..., please? Could I ..., please? May I ..., please? Is it OK / alright if I + present simple? Would it be OK / alright if I + past simple?	Yes, of course. Please do. By all means. Sorry, I'm afraid not. I'm afraid you can't. Sorry.

Do you mind if I + present simple? Would you mind if I + past simple?	No, not at all. Of course not. Please do. Sorry. I'm afraid you can't.

Work in pairs. Using the expressions above, ask for permission and respond.
Ask your partner if you can ...

1 borrow his/her pen.
2 look up a word in his/her dictionary.
3 copy his/her homework.
4 sit next to him/her next lesson.
5 go to his/her house after school.

Listening comprehension

1 🎧 2.12 Listen to a conversation and answer the questions.

1 How many people are speaking? Who are they?
2 Where does the conversation take place?
3 What is the situation?

2 🎧 2.12 Listen again and answer these questions. Make notes as you listen.

1 What sort of journey did Lisa have?
2 What did she lose on the train?
3 Who does she think took it? Why?
4 Why does Lisa want to phone her mum?
5 Why does Brenda ask Bob to carry Lisa's bags upstairs?
6 Is Bob looking forward to dinner? Why?
7 Why can't Lisa eat the roast chicken?
8 What does Lisa want to do before dinner? Why?
9 Is she thirsty? How do you know?
10 What sort of drink will she have?

Now share your answers with the rest of the class.

3 Talk about it.

1 How would you describe Uncle Bob and Aunt Brenda?
2 Do you have aunts and uncles? What are they like?

Writing features

Informing and explaining

> The article *Human achievement – spaceflight* is a piece of writing that **informs** and **explains**. It gives the reader information about spaceflight and explains how a rocket engine works, and how the shuttle was launched.

Checklist
Look again at the article *Human achievement – spaceflight* on pages 84 and 85.

▶ **Information and explanation**

You will often find *information* and *explanation* in the same piece of writing. *Human achievement – spaceflight* begins with information about the history of spaceflight followed by explanations of how a rocket engine works and the launch of the shuttle.

The information is under three subheadings. What are the subheadings?
Find examples of three pieces of information.
There are two sections of explanation. What are the subheadings?

▶ **Tenses**

Explanations are usually written in *present tenses*.
Find three examples of present tenses.

Sometimes, an explanation is written in *past tenses*. This is when what is being explained no longer happens. The space shuttle stopped flying in 2011, so the explanation is in past tenses.
Find three examples of past tenses in the explanation.

▶ **Sequence**

Explanations are written in the *order* that things happen, e.g. First, the fuels are combined …
Reread *How was the shuttle launched?* and pick out linking words and phrases that show you the order in which things happened.

▶ **Cause and effect**

In explanations, 'something' *causes* 'something else' to happen. Linking words and phrases help to show this, e.g. They were recovered by the US Navy so that they could be reused …
Find another example of a linking phrase.

▶ **Passive voice**

Explanations often use the *passive voice*, e.g. They were sent by the USA to the edge of space …
Find two more examples of the passive voice in the text.

▶ **Specialised vocabulary**

An explanation, especially a scientific one, will use *vocabulary* connected with the specialised subject, e.g. chemical reaction, orbital spacecraft.
Find five more examples of specialised vocabulary in the text.

▶ **Diagrams and captions**

It is often useful to use *diagrams* and *captions* to explain how something happens.
Discuss the diagrams and captions in the section *How does a rocket engine work?*
Do you find them useful? Why? / Why not?

Writing assignment
You have read and discussed a piece of writing that informs and explains. You are now going to write a short piece which gives the reader information and explains how something happens. You can research and write about either how a hot-air balloon gets off the ground or how the shuttle came back to Earth.

Go to p88 in your Workbook for help with your planning.

Life skills 2

Formal letter writing

As you get older, there will be times in your life when you need to write a **formal letter**. This may be to apply for a job, request information, complain, etc. The thing to remember is that a formal letter should be polite, well-organised and well-presented.

Bay City International School — ①

20.01.13 — ②

③ — Dr Helmut Feldman
Conductor, Klein Chamber Orchestra
14–16 Field Street
London
NW1 6TT

④ — Dear Dr Feldman

I am writing to inquire if your chamber orchestra would be able to perform at our International Arts festival to be held in July. Your nephew Gustav, who is involved in putting together the music programme, suggested we approach you about this matter. — ⑤

The programme for the festival is wide-ranging, including literature, poetry, dance, film and, of course, music. Within the music programme, we are catering for every taste with jazz, pop, indie, folk and classical concerts. There will be opportunities for students to perform but we are keen to include professional musicians of the highest calibre.

⑥ — Gustav has informed the festival committee that you are a small, London-based orchestra with an international reputation, and that the reviews for your most recent performance at the Berlin festival reported it as a triumph. We have been able to listen to some of your recordings and the entire committee is in agreement that the music programme would be greatly improved if you agree to take part.

Should you be able to perform, we can offer a concert hall that can hold 750 people and a date, within the week of the festival, to be arranged at your convenience.

⑦ — As I am sure you understand, putting together a festival of this size takes a great deal of organisation and we would be most grateful if you could let us know if you would be available as soon as possible, and what the fee would be for such a performance. If you would like any further information, please do not hesitate to contact us.

⑧ — Yours sincerely,
⑨ — *Lucie Duval*
LUCIE DUVAL (Miss)
Bay City International Festival Committee

A formal letter is set out in a certain style and uses formal language.

- It should be block paragraphed with a line between each paragraph.
- The use of informal language and contractions should be avoided.

Read each section of the letter with these notes.

1 Write your address in the top right-hand corner of the first page.

2 Write the date clearly.

3 This is the name and address of the person you are writing to – the recipient. Leave a line under the date. Go across to the left-hand side and write the recipient's address.

4 The greeting:
- *Dear Sir or Madam* – used when you do not know the name of the person you are writing to.
- *Dear [name]* – in formal letters it is usual to address the person using their title and name, e.g. *Mr Williams / Doctor Carter / Mrs Hill*. If you are writing to a woman and you do not know if she is married or not, use *Ms*.

5 First paragraph: Keep the first paragraph short and to the point, so the recipient knows exactly what the letter is about.

6 The body of the letter: Set out clearly what information you think the recipient needs to know. Don't be vague – give as much detail as possible.

7 Final paragraph: Make it clear what action you would like the recipient to take after having read your letter.

8 The ending:
- *Yours faithfully* if you do not know the person's name.
- *Yours sincerely* if you do know the person's name.

9 Your signature: Sign the letter, then print your name in capitals. Put your title (*Miss, Mr*, etc.) in brackets after your printed name. If you are writing on behalf of an organisation, print the name at the end.

Discuss:
What do you understand by the term 'block paragraph'? What other style of paragraphing is there? Where would you normally see this style?
Why do you think you should avoid informal language and contractions in a formal letter?

1 Why do you write your address on the letter?

2 What are the various ways of writing the date? Which do you think is the most appropriate for a formal letter?

3 Why do you think the recipient's name and address is on the letter?

4 Just as we use the abbreviations *Mr* [*Mister*]; *Mrs* [originally *Mistress*], we abbreviate other titles. How would you abbreviate:
- Doctor?
- Professor?

5 Read the first paragraph and discuss why Lucie is writing the letter.

6 Discuss the body of the letter:
- How many paragraphs are there?
- What is each paragraph about?
- Why do you think Lucie uses such phrases as *professional musicians of the highest calibre; reported it as a triumph*?

7 In the final paragraph, what action does Lucie want him to take?

8 Why does she end the letter *Yours sincerely*?

9 Why do you think:
- it is a good idea to print your name as well as signing the letter?
- you should put the name of the organisation as well as your individual name?

WB p122

Life skills 2: formal letter writing

It's an issue

Start-up Use WB p93 for your notes.

▼ Poverty exists across the world. Some people want to try to end it but others think that poor people will always exist, so not much can be done about it.

▲ Equality is regarded as a human right but not everyone agrees that laws should be made to ensure equal opportunities for everyone.

▲ Some people say that animals have the right to be treated kindly. Others say that they aren't the same as people so they don't matter in the same way.

Which of these issues have you discussed before?
Which ones have you heard discussed by other people or read about?
Which of them do you have a strong opinion about?
Are there any you have never heard of? Are there any you have no opinion about?

Reading

- You will read a discursive essay about cars. What does *discursive* mean?
  Why do you think it is important to learn to discuss things?

Vocabulary

- These words are in the essay: *automobile   contributor   respiratory   premature   campaigner   congestion.* Circle any you cannot remember or guess. Look them up.
- Find out what these phrases mean: *ozone layer   greenhouse gases   exhaust fumes   ultraviolet rays.*

Grammar

- You will study other changes that sometimes need to be made in **reported speech**.
  Think of two classes of word that you already know about changing in reported speech.

Word focus

- Dictionary: You will study how **words in definitions** are sometimes shown in **bold** type.
  What is the purpose of putting words in bold? What other treatment can be used?
- Spelling: You will revise words ending *-f* / *-fe*. Think of two words with each ending.
- Suffixes: You will learn about simple past tense endings of verbs.
  How many different sounds do the endings of these verbs have:
  walked   played   ended   washed   opened?

▼ Many people believe that climate change results from human activity and we should change aspects of our lives. Others say it is a natural event, so no changes are needed.

9

▲ Big companies buy a lot of land for growing food in huge quantities but some people think that the land used by small-scale farmers should be protected from these companies.

Grammar in use
- You will hear a discussion about the first day of the festival. **What three events would you include in the first day of the festival?**
- You will study the correct **order of adjectives**. **Think of adjectives in each of these categories: size, shape, colour, age, material.**

Listening and speaking
- You will listen to Professor Barnes, the archaeologist who is giving a talk at the festival. **Liam told Kurt about the professor's latest dig. Which country was it in?**
- You will prepare a presentation on an interesting discovery. **Are you most interested in discoveries in archaeology, history, science or nature? Why?**

Conversation focus 🎧 2.13
Florence is printing out an essay in the computer room when Liam arrives.
1. Listen to their conversation.
2. Read the questions on Workbook page 93. Listen again and answer the questions.
3. Talk in a group about the issues on this page and any other issues that are important to you. Use the photos to help you, as well as any of your own ideas.
   Ask: *What do you think about …? Isn't it true that …? Did you know …?*
   Say: *My view is …, I know other people think … but I'm completely sure that …, Some people say …*

Writing
- You will write your own discursive essay on either the subject of fashion or computer games. **Which of these do you have the strongest views about? Why?**

▲ Modern media bring benefits but some people think that too much time is spent in front of TVs and computers, so people become unfit and unsociable.

95

The Age of the Automobile

The car has become the most popular means of transport in the history of the world. Some people could not imagine life without a car. Others say that the world would be better off without them.

Since Karl Benz introduced the first automobile powered by a gasoline engine in 1885, many people see a car as a necessity in their lives rather than a luxury. Benz began selling his motorcar in 1888. In the five-year period from 1888 to 1893, 25 were sold. In 2007, when sales were at their peak, 54,920,317 cars were sold worldwide. Certainly, owning a car has many advantages but shouldn't we be concerned about the disadvantages? The number of cars on the road is a real problem and, as that number increases, the problem gets worse.

The first, and probably the greatest problem, is that of pollution. The fuel exhaust fumes from a car's engine contain many chemicals or emissions, such as carbon dioxide (CO_2), sulphur dioxide and lead. Nine hundred million metric tons of CO_2 is released into the atmosphere every year. This is a major contributor to air pollution, causing an increase in greenhouse gases and a decrease in the ozone layer. Greenhouse gases build up in the atmosphere and act like a blanket, trapping the sun's heat and causing the planet to warm up. We can see the results of this in more wildfires, extreme heatwaves and the melting of the polar ice caps, causing sea levels to rise. The ozone layer protects us from the sun's harmful ultraviolet rays. Car emissions contribute to the thinning of the ozone layer that decreases our protection. In the USA, for example, car emissions are the second largest source of CO_2. It is madness to think we can just go on producing more and more cars and ignore the damage being done.

Cars' emissions also cause severe health problems. When emissions are breathed in, they are carried by the bloodstream around the body and can do serious damage. They are particularly harmful to the respiratory system. It has been estimated that in the UK, 24,000 premature deaths every year are caused by air pollution. In Holland, a study was carried out on 632 children aged seven to 11. It was found that respiratory problems worsened as air pollution increased.

Further health problems, such as diabetes and obesity, occur because of lack of exercise. Obesity in children has been increasing and part of the cause is that they are taken everywhere by car! Walking and cycling are much healthier options. Many local councils and schools are working together to ensure that walking or cycling to school can be a safe, enjoyable experience. Surely, if parents are concerned about their children's health, they should leave the car at home and encourage their children to use their own two legs?

A further disadvantage of the car is the dependence on oil. Already, sensitive environmental areas of the world have been invaded by the oil industry and drilling has started as supplies elsewhere begin to dry up. The impact on the Arctic is a real concern. Peter Wadhams, Professor of Ocean Physics at Cambridge University has spent a long time there studying the problem. He said, "If there is a serious oil spill under ice in the Arctic, it will be very hard, if not impossible, to stop it becoming an environmental catastrophe." Wouldn't we be foolish to ignore his warning? Just look at what happened at the Deepwater Horizon Platform in the Gulf of Mexico in 2010! Five million barrels of harmful, dirty, black oil were released into the sea and it took three months to get it under control. Environmentalists said that the oil spill had happened the year before due to greed and carelessness. Have we learnt nothing? Ben Ayliffe, a polar campaigner for Greenpeace said that a spill in the Arctic would essentially make dealing with something like Deepwater Horizon look almost straightforward. The *Guardian* newspaper held a poll in August 2010, asking *Should drilling for oil be banned in sensitive environmental areas?* A huge 85.7 per cent of people who took part said that it should be banned and those areas should be protected at all costs. I would like to know how many of that 85.7 per cent actually do something about it by giving up their cars or, at least, using them as little as possible.

There are many people, of course, who will argue that having a car is a necessity. People who live in remote, rural communities, for example. Without a car, how would they get from place to place? They do have a point but the solution lies not in every member of the family having a car and using it several times a day but in an improved, cheap and efficient public transport service. Governments are always 'talking' about improving public transport but talking is about all they do. If the problem of the increasing number of cars on the road is to be addressed, then money has to be spent on better bus and rail systems.

You will be told that one of the major advantages is individual freedom. You can get in your car whenever you like and travel to wherever you like. You can go door-to-door without worrying about whether the train is on time or whether you will have to stand in the freezing cold at a bus stop. It sounds like a very good argument but is it? When you consider the harm that the motorcar is doing to the planet, people's health and the natural environment, the congestion in our towns and cities, the horrific motorway pile-ups – ask yourselves this, is it really such a hardship to have to wait for a bus or a train to come along?

The motorcar seems to be here to stay – at least until the oil runs out – but there are things we MUST do to slow down the damage. Car sharing, greater use of public transport and greater investment in alternatives such as electric cars would greatly help the situation. Doing nothing is not an option. The problems are here NOW and they are increasing. Next time you are about to get in your car, stop and think: Do I really have to drive? Consider the alternatives. A brisk walk, an energetic cycle or use of public transport would be beneficial to you and the planet!

Reading comprehension

1 **Discuss these questions.**

1. In what year did Karl Benz introduce the first gasoline-powered automobile?
2. How many cars were sold from 1888 to 1893?
3. What do car emissions:
   a increase in the atmosphere?
   b decrease in the atmosphere?
4. Find an example of a health problem caused by car emissions.
5. Where have the oil industry started drilling for oil?
6. Who does Ben Ayliffe work for?
7. What happened in the Gulf of Mexico in 2010?
8. Give two examples of what can be done to stop the increase in cars on the road.

2 **Match the phrases in the box to the correct definition.**

| begin to dry up | a real concern | individual freedom |
| look almost straightforward | not an option | beneficial to you |

1. _____ not a choice we have
2. _____ decrease and disappear
3. _____ for your own good
4. _____ something to worry about
5. _____ seem simple
6. _____ being able to do what you want

3 **Discuss the discursive style of the essay.**

1. List the advantages and disadvantages the writer discusses in the essay.
2. Look at your lists.
   a Do you think the writer supports or does not support the use of the car?
   b Look at each 'advantage'. What does the writer have to say about each one?
3. By using the phrases below what opinion about cars does the writer want the reader to have?

> ... the problem gets worse ...   It is madness to think ...   Have we learnt nothing?
> Surely, if parents are concerned about their children's health ...   ... be foolish to ignore his warning?
> ... is it really such a hardship ...   Doing nothing is not an option.

4. What does the writer suggest that readers do in the final paragraph?

4 **Discuss your answers to these questions.**

1. What examples does the writer use to support the view that the planet is warming up?
2. Why do you think parents might not want their children walking or cycling to school?
3. In what ways do you think 'greed and carelessness' were the reasons for the oil spill in the Gulf of Mexico?
4. Why do you think the writer would like to know 'how many of that 85.7 per cent actually do something about it by giving up their cars or, at least, using them as little as possible'?

5 **What do you think?**

- Do you agree or disagree with the writer's point of view? Explain your reasons.
- Which do you think is the strongest reason for decreasing the number of cars on the road? Why?
- Which do you think is the best suggestion to decrease the number of cars on the road?

Grammar

1 Read.

Last month there was a debate on television entitled *The Age of the Automobile*. A panel of experts and a studio audience expressed strong views about the advantages and disadvantages of cars.

- Car emissions cause health problems. **These problems** are getting worse all the time.
- I gave up driving a car **last year**.
- There was a terrible traffic jam **yesterday**.
- We need to ban cars from city centres **here and now**!
- I bought my first car **a month ago**. I can't do without it.

A surprising number of people were against cars. Many people said that car emissions caused health problems and that **those problems** were getting worse all the time. One man said that he had given up driving a car **the year before**. A young woman reported that there had been a terrible traffic jam in her town **the previous day**. An older woman shouted that they needed to ban cars from city centres **there and then**. After all this criticism of cars, a young man stood up and said that he had bought his first car **a month before** and that he couldn't do without it.

2 Cover the text in Activity 1 above. Write *True* or *False*. Correct the false statements.

1. Not many people were against cars. ....
2. A number of people knew about the health risks caused by cars. ....
3. Everyone in the audience had a car. ....
4. An older woman shouted that cars should be banned from city centres immediately. ....
5. Nobody was in favour of cars. ....

3 Complete the reported sentences with the words and phrases from the box.

the previous day	the following week
the next day	the week before
three weeks before	that day

1. "I'm going to buy a new car next week." He said that he was going to buy a new car ....
2. "I went to Paris three weeks ago." She said that she had gone to Paris ....
3. "We saw a good film yesterday." They said that they had seen a good film ....
4. "There's a cold wind today." She said that there was a cold wind ....
5. "I'll finish my work tomorrow." He said that he would finish his work ....
6. "We had an exam last week." They said that they had had an exam ....

4 Report these statements.

1. "I lost my mobile yesterday." She said ...
2. "I don't like these photos." He said ...
3. "I learnt to swim last year." He said ...
4. "We saw this film two months ago." They said ...
5. "I'll phone John tomorrow." She said ...
6. "We saw a rabbit here in our garden." They said ...
7. "We're leaving now." He said ...

Changes in reported speech

this and **these** change to **that** and **those**.
He said, "I like **this** shirt but not **these** jeans."
He said that he liked **that** shirt but not **those** jeans.
here becomes **there**.
"We live **here**," they said.
They said that they lived **there**.
Adverbs of time change when statements are reported on a different day.
She said, "I feel ill **today**."
She said that she felt ill **that day**.
tomorrow → the following day, the next day
yesterday → the day before, the previous day
next week → the following week, the week after
last year → the year before, the previous year
two months ago → two months before
now → then
These adverbs do not change when statements are reported on the same day.
"It's my birthday **today**," she said.
She said it was her birthday **today**.

Word focus

A Dictionary work — Bold words in the definition

If a word in a definition also has an entry of its own, it is in bold.

> fuel¹   [ˈfjuːəl]   noun
>
> 1 [C / U] SCIENCE a substance such as oil, gas, coal or wood that releases energy when it is burned. Coal and wood are sometimes called **solid fuel**.
> 2 [U] petrol or **diesel** used in vehicles

So if you are puzzled about the meaning of **solid fuel** or **diesel**, you can look them up for further explanation.

1 These words all appear in the discursive essay. Look up each word in the dictionary and write the bold word in each definition.

> pollution   carbon dioxide   lead (n)

2 Look up the bold word in each definition to ensure you understand its meaning.

B Spelling — Revision: plurals of words ending in -f / -fe

> Some words ending in -f just add -s, e.g.
> gulf → gulfs
> Some words ending in -f or -fe change to -ves in the plural, e.g.
> life → lives

Use your dictionary to write the plurals of these words. Remember: if it is just -s, then the plural will not be given. If the plural is -ves, it will be shown.

1 cliff   2 loaf   3 roof
4 half   5 wife   6 shelf
7 yourself 8 staff   9 thief

C Word groups — Specialised subjects

These words are in the discursive essay:

> pollution fuel carbon dioxide atmosphere
> lead sulphur dioxide ultraviolet diabetes
> bloodstream greenhouse gas respiratory

Group the words together under these specialised subject labels.

> environment   science   physics
> chemistry   biology   health

Some will be in more than one group. Use your dictionary to help you.

D Suffixes — -ed / -d/ -t

> The suffix -ed is usually used to form the past tense of a verb, e.g.
> happen → happened
> Some verbs form the past tense with -t instead of -ed, e.g.
> spend → spent
> Some verbs can have either ending, e.g.
> learn → learnt / learned

1 Form the past tense of these verbs. Remember, some can have both endings.

1 consider   2 leap   3 send
4 dream   5 argue   6 spell
7 kneel   8 ask   9 spoil
10 burn   11 ignore 12 spill

2 Choose four of the past tenses you have formed in Activity 1. Use them in sentences of your own.

Grammar in use

Good luck, everyone!

1 🎧 2.15 Listen and read.

Todd: Hi, guys! All set? The gates open any minute now.
Ramon: The **Super Silver Jazz** Band is already playing by the entrance.
Tasha: And the traditional dancers are waiting backstage in the hall.
Lucie: Have you seen those **gorgeous, purple, Indian** costumes?
Ramon: I noticed the sculptures are back in the garden.
Rudi: Yes, they weren't stolen after all. They were in the gym!
Ramon: What? How come?
Rudi: Mr Collins, the caretaker, moved them. He was worried they would be damaged by last night's thunderstorm.
Tasha: How on earth did he manage to move that **huge, metal** horse?
Lucie: And why is there a **massive, red and yellow** tent on the playing field?
Tasha: That's for the kids' circus skills this afternoon.
Rudi: There really is something for everyone.
Todd: Professor Barnes is giving his talk this evening: *Art and Archaeology*.
Lucie: And then, of course, after that it's *The River Boys*.
Ramon: Wow! What a way to end the first day of the festival!
Todd: OK, guys. Time to take our places! Good luck, everyone!

2 Answer these questions.

1 When is the festival going to start?
2 How many events are happening today?
3 Why did the caretaker move the sculptures?
4 What is the tent on the playing field for?
5 Why does Rudi say that there is 'something for everyone'?

3 Match two adjectives from the box to each of the groups below.

round	tiny	swimming	crimson
triangular	interesting	old	turquoise
Chinese	enormous	silk	Mexican
horrible	dancing	new	plastic

opinion	size	age	shape

colour	origin	material	purpose

4 Put the adjectives in front of the nouns in the correct order.

1 flowers (scarlet, tiny)
2 a wall (high, stone)
3 a table (huge, circular)
4 a painting (Japanese, fascinating)
5 a coat (black, velvet, long)
6 a guitar (Spanish, beautiful, old)
7 coins (ancient, Greek, valuable, gold)
8 a boat (old, fishing, white, strange, black)

5 Make up your own sentences using two or more adjectives from Activity 3 with the nouns below.

1 a chair   2 a necklace
3 a car   4 a sculpture
5 costumes 6 shoes
7 paintings 8 books

1 *He bought a horrible, turquoise, plastic chair.*

Order of adjectives

When adjectives precede the noun, they usually appear in this order:

opinion + size + age + shape + colour + origin + material + purpose

*a **sweet, little** child* (opinion + size)
***purple, Indian** silk* (colour + origin)
***strange, old, green, leather, walking** boots*
(opinion + age + colour + material + purpose)
Adjectives before a noun are separated by commas. *an **unusual, tiny, gold** ring*
When adjectives are from the same group, insert *and*. *a **massive, red and yellow** tent*

Grammar in use: the order of adjectives before nouns

Listening and speaking

Listening comprehension
You are going to hear part of the talk which Professor Barnes, the archaeologist, gave to the festival audience and look at some of the photos which he showed them.

1. 🎧 2.16 Listen and explain in your own words the connection between Tutankhamun and the Chrysler Building in New York.

2. 🎧 2.16 Listen again and write *T* (true), *F* (false) or *NS* (not stated).
    1. Howard Carter made the discovery in 1932. ....
    2. Tutankhamun's tomb was discovered in the Valley of the Kings. ....
    3. He returned to England because he had run out of money. ....
    4. The contents of the tomb included food and drink. ....
    5. The contents of the tomb are on display in Cairo. ....
    6. The discovery made Howard Carter a rich man. ....
    7. News of the discovery spread all over the world. ....
    8. People quickly became bored with the style of Ancient Egypt. ....
    9. Architecture in the 1920s was heavily influenced by that of Ancient Egypt. ....
    10. The sun was important in the religion of Ancient Egypt. ....
    11. In the 1920s, all Egyptian-style items were extremely expensive. ....
    12. Tutankhamun lived five thousand years ago. ....

    Correct the false statements. Talk about the statements which you marked *NS* (not stated). Why did you choose these answers?

3. Talk about the photos which Professor Barnes showed his audience. Describe them. Were they a good choice? What do you think of the styles of the 1920s and 30s?

Individual speaking
You are going to talk about an interesting discovery.
Preparation in groups:

1. Make a list of all the interesting discoveries you can think of. These may be archaeological or historical or they could be discoveries of other kinds, e.g. natural discoveries or scientific discoveries.
2. What do you know about these discoveries? When and where did they happen? Who made the discoveries?
3. How important are these discoveries today? What influence have they had on our daily lives?

Now tell the rest of the class about your discussion. **WB p99**

Writing features

Discursive essay

> *The Age of the Automobile* is a **discursive** essay. The writer looks at the advantages and disadvantages of the increasing number of cars, and expresses her opinion that something must be done about the problem.

Checklist
Look again at *The Age of the Automobile* on pages 96 and 97.

▸ **Subject**
A discursive essay is a piece of writing that expresses a personal opinion about a particular *subject*.
What is the subject of *The Age of the Automobile*? What is the writer's opinion?

▸ **Purpose**
A discursive essay has a particular *purpose*.
Discuss the purpose of *The Age of the Automobile*.
How is the writer hoping readers will react?

▸ **Opening paragraph**
The *first paragraph* of a discursive piece of writing must make it clear to the reader what is being discussed and the attitude of the writer, i.e. which side of the argument he/she is on.
Explain how the writer does this in the opening paragraph.

▸ **For and against**
In discursive writing, the writer must look at *both sides* of the argument.
Look at paragraphs 2 to 5. Discuss what the writer argues are the disadvantages.
Why does the writer use four paragraphs?
Look at paragraphs 6 and 7. What advantages does the writer consider and what reasons does she give for dismissing them? Why does the writer use two paragraphs?

▸ **Final paragraph**
The *final paragraph* of discursive writing summarises the points that have been made before and comes to a conclusion. It can also make an appeal to the reader.
What points does the writer repeat to show that something must be done about the problem? What appeal does she make to the reader?

▸ **Persuasive language**
Obviously, the writer wants readers to agree with her point of view. She uses very *positive persuasive language* when she is discussing alternatives to the motorcar, e.g. **healthier option, cheap and efficient public transport system**.
She uses very *negative persuasive language* when she is discussing the disadvantages of the motorcar, e.g. **a real problem; harmful, dirty, black oil**.
Find other examples of persuasive language in the essay.

▸ **Appeal to readers**
The writer wants readers to agree with her opinion. She *appeals* to them by asking direct questions which they should think about, e.g. **Wouldn't we be foolish to ignore his warning?**
Find other examples of questions in the essay that ask readers to stop and think.

▸ **Facts**
The writer uses *facts* to support her opinion, e.g. **In 2007, when sales were at their peak, 54,920,317 cars were sold worldwide**.
Find other examples of facts used to support the writer's opinion.

Writing assignment
You have read and discussed the discursive essay *The Age of the Automobile*.
You are now going to write a discursive essay on <u>one</u> of the following:
- Some people believe it is important to look nice but others say we spend too much time on appearance and fashion.
What are your views on this statement?
- Some people enjoy playing computer games but others say it would be better to spend free time on physical activities.
What are your views on this statement?

> *Go to p100 in your Workbook for help with your planning.*

Influences

Start-up *Use WB p103 for your notes.*

▲ When people are growing up, they are influenced by those around them. Autobiographies often recount early influences.

◀ Families are important influences, not just parents but brothers, sisters and grandparents.

▲ Teachers often have a long-lasting influence on students. Many successful people remember how a particular teacher inspired them.

Are you more influenced by people inside or outside of your family?
What do you think are the best kind of influences?
Are heroes always good influences? Why? / Why not?
What do you think of as being bad influences?
What do you do about them?

Reading
- You will read an autobiographical extract in which the writer recounts two very different influences from his school days. **Think of three features you would expect the writer to use in a piece of autobiographical writing.**

Vocabulary
- These words are in the extract: *atmosphere   old-fashioned   respect   pointless   demonstrate.* **Circle any you cannot remember or guess. Look them up.**
- Find out what these phrases mean: *my heart sank   not a care in the world.*

Grammar
- You will study **would to express habitual actions in the past**. What is a habit?

Word focus
- Dictionary: You will learn where synonyms and antonyms are sometimes shown in a dictionary definition. **Define *antonym* and *synonym*.**
- Spelling: You will look at letters that disappear from the endings of some words when a suffix is added. **Look at this noun: *adventure*. What is the adjective?**
- Suffixes: You will look at adjectives formed with *-ive*. **Think of two that you already know the meanings of: 1) 'very big' and 2) 'nice to look at'.**

10

▲ Friends are important in most people's lives. Who we spend time with when we are young can influence the rest of our lives.

▲ In the classic novel, *Oliver Twist*, Dickens showed how thieves influenced poor boys into becoming thieves themselves.

Grammar in use
- You will hear a conversation on the last day of the festival. **What do you think would be a good way to end the festival?**
- You will learn about **causative expressions**. **How often do you get your teeth checked by a dentist? Where do you have your hair cut?**

Listening and speaking
- You will practise making suggestions and giving advice. **Are you better at giving advice or listening to advice from other people?**
- You will listen to a conversation in which a girl gets advice about a problem she has in school. **Think of three different problems the girl might want advice about.**

Conversation focus 🎧 2.17
Everyone is enjoying the festival. The students were particularly impressed by Professor Barnes.
1. Listen to their conversation in the festival café.
2. Read the questions on Workbook page 103. Listen again and answer the questions.
3. Talk in a group about things that influence you. Use the photos to help you, as well as any of your own ideas. Ask: *Who do you admire? Who inspires you? Who do you try to be / not to be like?* Say: *I always listen to what … says, I want / don't want to be like …, I'm inspired by …*

▲ Ghandi's belief in non-violent opposition to injustice influenced Nelson Mandela, prisoner for 25 years but president of South Africa 1994–99 and the hero of many.

Writing
- You will write an autobiographical extract about a person in your past who had an effect on you. **Think of three different aspects of a person that you can describe in order to show their character.**

105

Leo

I remember the first time I saw Leo. I was just 14 and it was the beginning of my third year at Sun Hill School. It was a freezing cold day and I was hanging around in the coldest corner of the playground, trying not to be noticed, as usual, and feeling miserable.

My first two years at the school had been disastrous, at least I thought so. I was younger and smaller than the rest of the boys and cleverer than most of them, though I tried not to show it. I had spent two years trying to hide my ideas, my thoughts, my interests and, in fact, myself from Danny Liddle, the source of my misery, from whom I was hiding on that wintry day in the coldest corner of the playground.

Danny was a tough guy, large and imposing. He bought his clothes in the smartest shops. He got his hair cut in the latest style and it looked good. He was cool. He was a leader – in a way. Most boys didn't like him but they let him do his own thing because they didn't dare to stop him or didn't know how to. His influence in the class was strong and the atmosphere was intimidating. At the beginning he didn't notice me but after I came first in class tests a few times and then regularly, I was aware his eye was on me. One day he called to me across the playground. I hesitated in alarm and he didn't like it. It looked like defiance. I'm surprised he didn't recognise fear. He came over with one of his friends and glared at me, demanding respect but all he got was the trembling glance of a frightened rabbit. He didn't mistake that. I was clearly someone he could use to stay on top. I could see him thinking it all through. He wasn't intelligent but he was cunning.

He got into the habit of making nasty remarks about me within the hearing of other boys. It might be what I was wearing or my old-fashioned school bag that my grandmother had given me. "Hey, Robbie, don't you know what an idiot you look?" he'd say. Or he'd tell everyone how pointless my latest project was. Nobody stood up for me and I didn't stand up for myself. Danny could say what he liked and nobody would contradict him. Although I tried to keep out of his way, he always hunted me down. Whenever I did well, he would be there beside me, jeering and sneering to the amusement of his friends. Although I was the most successful student in the class, nobody looked up to me because Danny didn't. He controlled the way everyone else treated me. However much I succeeded, I felt a failure. Nothing compensated for feeling like a helpless victim.

That's how it was when Leo arrived. When I first saw him, he was casually chatting to other boys, friendly and relaxed, looking like he enjoyed life and hadn't a care in the world. He was tall and strongly built. He didn't look as though he could ever be pushed around by someone like Danny, which was interesting, as one of the boys he was talking to was Danny. Danny was laughing. He glanced across the playground at me, and said something to Leo and laughed again. Leo looked in my direction. My heart sank. Two of them to deal with, I thought. I can't bear it.

The bell went for the start of school. I'd have to go in. I'd have to walk past them. I knew what was going to happen. Danny was going to show this new boy how to treat me. He would demonstrate his power to humiliate me in front of everyone. As I came level with them, Danny said, "This is the clown who carries his books in a kid's bag. He belongs in the kindergarten!" I felt my throat tighten and the tears start at the back of my eyes. I swallowed hard. I just wanted to get past. Danny was barring my way, waiting for an approving laugh from his new friend. It didn't come.

Instead Leo just said, "Danny says it's your project on display in the hall." I looked at him, waiting for the derisive comment. Leo said, "I've seen it. It's great. Really interesting." That was all. I stared at him. Danny stared at him. Then we all moved silently inside.

Leo's arrival had a stunning impact on our class. Not straight away, but little by little, the atmosphere changed. Danny's silly comments in class one day didn't get an admiring laugh from the other boys. One day I noticed that it wasn't just me who was answering questions but other boys were joining in. I no longer felt ridiculous for producing good work. When Danny tried to assert himself by mocking me, Leo would turn up at my side. He didn't do anything. He didn't say anything. He just looked at Danny and Danny would shuffle off. I had thought so many times about what I'd do to Danny if I was bigger. Leo was bigger but he didn't do any of them. You might have thought that two giants would need to fight it out. Eventually I realised that Leo didn't need to use his strength like that. Just being the way he was was enough to make Danny back down. Danny had used his strength to intimidate because, deep down, he was afraid that people wouldn't respect him and because of that, they never had. His power vanished like morning mist.

Leo wasn't the cleverest and he wasn't the best sportsman or artist but everything he did, he did to the best of his ability. Gradually, I realised that was what gave him confidence. One warm spring day, sitting in a sunny corner of the playground, I told him what a difference he had made to me. He just smiled and said, "Everybody should have the freedom to do the best they can in the best way they can. Nobody should take that away from anyone. It's a firm belief of mine. You've got talent so let it shine." After that I started to believe in myself. My expectations for the future changed. Of course, Danny never bothered me again. Everything I have become and everything I have achieved I owe to Leo.

Reading comprehension

1 Discuss these questions.
1. What time of the year was it when Robbie first saw Leo?
2. How many years had Robbie already been at Sun Hill School before Leo arrived?
3. Who was the source of his misery?
4. Who had given Robbie his old-fashioned school bag?
5. Who was Leo talking to when Robbie first saw him?
6. Where did Danny say that Robbie belonged?
7. What did Leo say was really interesting?
8. How quickly did things change after Leo arrived?

2 Match the phrases to the meanings.
1. to be a tough guy ....
2. to be cool ....
3. to do your own thing ....
4. to have not a care in the world ....

a. to be considered by others as having good style and being fashionable
b. to behave in an individual way, not taking any notice of anyone else
c. to be completely free from worries
d. to be strong and not scared or worried by anyone else

3 Scan the text to find the answers to these questions.
1. What animal does Robbie use to describe himself when Danny first called to him across the playground? What impression of Robbie does this give you?
2. What person does Danny introduce Robbie to Leo as? Why do you think he uses this word?
3. What people does Robbie compare Leo and Danny to? Why do you think he describes them like this?
4. How does Robbie describe the way Danny's power disappeared? What does this tell you about Danny?

4 Discuss your answers to these questions.
1. How did Danny use Robbie to 'stay on top'?
2. What did Danny try to achieve by intimidating other boys?
3. Did the other boys respect Danny? How did they feel about him?
4. During the first two years did Danny stop Robbie from doing well at his work? How do you know?
5. Why do you think the boys stared at Leo when he said that Robbie's project was good?
6. Did Leo and Danny ever have a real fight? How do you know?
7. What might they have had a fight about?
8. How was the question answered?

5 What do you think?
- Do you think Robbie was right to keep trying to hide from Danny? Give your reasons.
- Robbie was at school for two years with Danny. Leo stopped Danny's behaviour in a few weeks. Which of them do you admire most? Explain your answer.
- Do you agree with Leo's belief? Why? / Why not?

Grammar

1 Read.

Danny Liddle was a bully who took pleasure in intimidating others. He got into the habit of making nasty comments about Robbie. He **would make fun of** his clothes or he **would laugh** at his old-fashioned school bag. Robbie tried to keep out of his way but Danny **would** always **hunt** him **down**. Robbie was an intelligent boy and worked hard at school. However, whenever he did well, Danny **would** always **be** there beside him jeering and sneering. However successful Robbie was, Danny made him feel a failure. When Leo arrived at school, things started to change. Little by little Danny began to lose the power he had once had over the class. When Danny tried to assert himself by mocking Robbie, Leo **would turn up** at his side. He would not say anything. He **would** just **look** at Danny until he shuffled off. It soon became clear that nobody respected Danny and his power vanished like morning mist.

2 Answer these questions.
1. What did Danny make fun of?
2. What happened when Robbie tried to keep out of Danny's way?
3. How did Danny react when Robbie did well?
4. How did this make Robbie feel?
5. After Leo's arrival how did things change?
6. How did Leo help Robbie?

3 Rewrite these sentences using *would* + infinitive (without *to*).
1. Danny Liddle bullied other boys.
   Danny Liddle would bully other boys.
2. He always made life difficult for Robbie.
3. Danny always wore fashionable clothes.
4. He mocked the way Robbie dressed.
5. He told Robbie that he looked stupid.
6. The other boys laughed at Robbie, too.
7. He used to sneer when Robbie did well in class.
8. Robbie always felt a failure.

4 Tick the box if the sentence can be changed to *would* + verb. Rewrite the sentences you ticked using *would* + infinitive (without *to*).
1. As a child, my father lived in the country. ☐
2. He had his own horse. ☐
3. He used to ride his horse every day. ☐
4. He was an only child. ☐
5. Sometimes he felt lonely. ☐
6. He used to escape from his loneliness in books. ☐

5 Think about your childhood. Write sentences using *would* + infinitive (without *to*). Discuss your sentences in pairs.
1. Think about things that you regularly did as a child. Write three sentences.
2. Think about things that your family would regularly do. Write three sentences.
3. Think about things that your primary school teachers would do. Write three sentences.

> We can use **would** + infinitive (**without to**) for actions which happened regularly in the past.
> *During the summer holidays we used to camp on the beach.* →
> *During the summer holidays we* **would camp** *on the beach.*
> *My brothers went fishing every day.* →
> *My brothers* **would go** *fishing every day.*
> *I often slept under the stars.* →
> *I* **would** *often* **sleep** *under the stars.*
> In speech we often use the short form of *would*.
> *Very often we* **'d light** *a fire.*
> *My father loved music. He* **'d** *always* **play** *the guitar and* **sing**.
> We cannot use *would* + infinitive (without *to*) when we are talking about continuing states in the past.
> *He used to live in London.*
> *Live* indicates a continuing state, not a repeated action, so using *would* is impossible here.

Grammar: *would* + infinitive (without *to*) to express habitual actions in the past

Word focus

A Dictionary work Synonyms and antonyms

Sometimes, within a definition, a synonym is given.

clever /ˈklevə(r)/ adj **1** good at learning or understanding things
= INTELLIGENT

Sometimes, within a definition, an antonym is given.

aware /əˈweər/ adj **1** knowing about a situation or fact
≠ UNAWARE

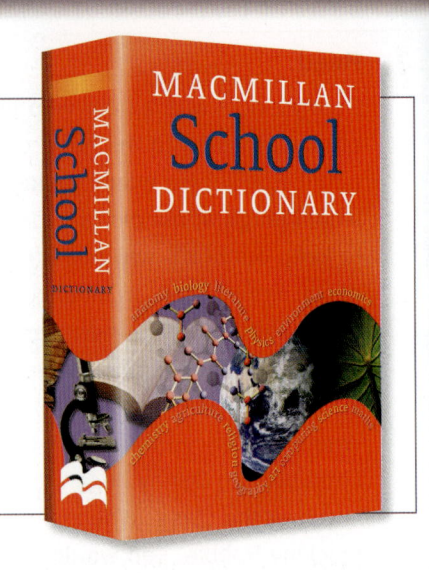

1 Use your dictionary to find the synonyms of these words from the extract.
   1 beginning   2 defiance   3 nasty   4 remark

2 Use your dictionary to find the antonyms of these words from the extract.
   1 most   2 succeed   3 approve   4 firm

B Spelling Disappearing letters

Sometimes when we add a suffix, a letter from the root word disappears, e.g.
disaster ⟶ disastrous
winter ⟶ wintry

Do these word sums. Remember, one letter from the root word will disappear. Use a dictionary to check your answers.

1 humour   + ous
2 wonder   + ous
3 glamour   + ous
4 generous   + ity
5 curious   + ity
6 hinder   + ance
7 remember   + ance
8 enter   + ance
9 repeat   + ition
10 exclaim   + ation

C Word groups
Scan the extract and find:
1 four comparative adjectives with -er.
2 four superlative adjectives with -est.
3 one superlative adjective with most.
4 four irregular past simple verbs.

D Suffixes -ive

The suffix -ive forms adjectives that show a quality or a tendency, e.g.
deride: to say that someone or something is stupid or useless
derisive: showing that you think someone or something is stupid or useless

1 Form the adjectives with -ive from these root words. Check spelling and meaning in your dictionary.
   1 appreciate   2 support   3 assert
   4 select   5 impress   6 persuade

2 Write the -ive adjectives to complete these statements. The word in bold is a clue.
   1 If something is **repeated**, it is ....
   2 If you **argue** a lot, you are ....
   3 If something **informs** you, it is ....
   4 If you **create** things, you are ....
   5 If you **talk** a lot, you are ....
   6 If you **support** someone, you are ....
   7 If you **compete**, you are ....
   8 If you are good at **imagining**, you are ....
   9 If you **respond** to someone, you are ....
   10 If something **impresses** you, it is ....

Grammar in use

1 Listen and read.

Lucie: What an amazing week!
Rudi: You're right. It's been fantastic.
Todd: And tonight's ballet performance was the perfect way to end the festival.
Tasha: The sound system broke down in rehearsal but we managed to **get** it **fixed** in time, thank goodness.
Ramon: I was surprised to see Eva on the stage.
Todd: One of the dancers had an injury, so Eva stood in for her.
Lucie: Her dress was fabulous.
Rudi: She **got** it **made** especially for tonight.
Tasha: Didn't Miss Jackson look lovely?
Lucie: Yes, she did. She'd **had** her hair **done** and everything.
Todd: Congratulations, everybody! The festival's been a huge success.
Ramon: It certainly has. Well done, everybody!
Rudi: We should **get** a photo **taken** of all the committee.
Todd: Good idea! Come on. Let's go outside. It's time for the grand finale.
Lucie: Thanks to Lee and his family.
Ramon: His father is so generous. He **had** the fireworks **flown over** from Hong Kong especially for tonight. They're going to be spectacular!
Rudi: And they're starting now! Come on! Let's go and watch!

2 Answer these questions.

1. Is tonight the first or last night of the festival?
2. What happened to the sound system? Did they get it fixed?
3. Why was Eva dancing in the ballet?
4. Why did Miss Jackson look lovely?
5. What was Rudi's good idea?
6. How will the festival close?

3 Make sentences as in the example. Use the past simple.

1. we – get – photo – take
   We got our photo taken.
2. my father – have – car – clean
3. we – have – house – paint
4. they – get – old tree – cut down
5. he – have – painful tooth – pull out
6. Miss Jackson – have – hair – do
7. Tasha – get – sound system – fix
8. Lee's father – have – fireworks – fly over

4 Make sentences as in the example. Use the verbs from the box.

| repair | frame | pull down |
| clean | cut | deliver |

1. John's hair is too long. What should he do?
   He should get it cut. Or: *He should have it cut.*
2. The car isn't working. What ought we to do?
3. The windows are very dirty. What will you do?
4. Jane ordered some flowers over the phone. She didn't pick them up from the shop herself. What did she do?
5. Mr Jones bought a very old house. He wanted to build a new one on that spot, so what did he do with the old one?
6. Sally took a lovely photo of her grandparents. She decided to give it to them as a present. What did she do with the photo?

In **causative constructions**, the subject of the sentence does not perform the action. The subject causes the action to happen.
*Jane **had** her photo **taken**.*
Jane is the subject but she did not take the photo herself. A photographer did.
*Danny **got** his hair **cut**.*
Danny is the subject but he did not cut his hair himself. A hairdresser did.
In causative constructions, we use *have* or *got* + past participle.

Look at the causatives in the dialogue in Activity 1 above. Say what the subject of each sentence is and suggest who might have performed the action.

Listening and speaking

Functions of English: making suggestions and giving advice

1 Look at these useful expressions.

> You should ...   You ought to ...   Why don't you ...?   If I were you, I would ...   I suggest + verb + -ing.
> I suggest that you ...   You could always ...   Perhaps you could ...
> It might be a good idea if you + past tense   Have you considered + verb + -ing?
> Have you thought about + verb + -ing?

2 Your friends have some simple problems. Read and make suggestions using the expressions in Activity 1.

1 "I don't know what this word means."
2 "I don't know anything about this topic."
3 "I've got a terrible headache."
4 "I love these shoes but they're worn out."

3 Here are some trickier problems. Make helpful suggestions using the expressions in Activity 1.

1 *It's my mum's birthday next week. I want to buy her a nice present but I haven't got any money. Any advice?*

2 *There's a girl in my class who's really mean. She's always making nasty remarks about me. I often feel like crying. What can I do?*

3 *I saw a boy in our class steal some money from a girl's bag. I don't know what to do. Can you help?*

4 *I'm finding my schoolwork really hard this year. I'm getting terrible marks and my parents are often cross with me. I really don't know what to do.*

4 Group conversation

First work in pairs. Make up a tricky problem that you and your partner have. Make notes.
Form groups. Find out what each other's problems are. Talk about the problems and give advice.

Listening comprehension

You are going to hear a girl talking to her mother.

1 🎧 Listen. What is Katie's problem?

1 She is ill.   2 She is lazy.   3 She is being bullied.

2 🎧 Listen again and answer the questions. Make notes.

1 According to Katie, why can't she go to school today?
2 Where does Katie's mum think they should go?
3 How much school has Katie missed this week?
4 What did Katie's mum hear Katie doing last night?
5 Who doesn't Katie like at school?
6 What does this girl make nasty comments about? Name four things.
7 What do the other girls do?
8 What does the girl do when Katie gets a question right?
9 What is Katie's mum's first piece of advice?
10 What is her second suggestion?
11 What is Katie afraid will happen?
12 Do you think Katie had a stomach ache? Why? / Why not?

3 Talk about it.

1 What do you think of the advice which Katie's mum gave to her daughter?
2 If Katie came to you for advice, what would you say to her?

Writing features

Autobiographical extract

Leo is an **autobiographical extract** in which the writer remembers people in his past who had a great effect on him. Remembering Danny makes him relive his misery and fear; remembering Leo makes him feel admiration and gratitude.

Checklist
Look again at *Leo* on pages 106 and 107.

▶ **Introduction**
The writer *begins* by making it very clear that what he is about to narrate is a personal experience and has happened in the past.
What words in the opening sentence make this clear?
It is important that the reader knows when and where.
What details in the opening paragraph let the reader know when and where?

▶ **First person**
Autobiographies are written in the *first person*.
Find examples of the first person in the extract.

▶ **Past tenses**
Autobiographies are written in *past tenses*.
Find examples of past tenses in the extract.

▶ **The plot**
Things that happen in real life can be called the *plot* just as in fiction. In the extract, the writer mentions several incidents which show how Danny makes his life a misery and how Leo changes all that.
Discuss what happens in the extract.

▶ **Precise detail: the people**
The writer uses *precise details* when he describes the characters of Danny and Leo.
The reader needs to know about the characters that have had such an effect on the writer. They have to be more than just names.
Danny is described as having the latest clothes. What else do we know about Danny's appearance?
Danny is described as tough. What else do we know about the type of person he is – his personality?
Leo is described as tall. What else do we know about Leo's appearance?
Leo is described as not having a care in the world. What else do we know about the type of person Leo is – his personality?

▶ **Precise detail: writer's thoughts and feelings**
So the reader can understand the type of person the writer is and how what happened affected him, he uses *precise details*.
He writes:
- the atmosphere was intimidating NOT *it was not very nice*.
- I felt a failure NOT *It bothered me a bit*.

Find the precise details the writer gives when:
- *Danny called him over in the playground.*
- *Danny came over and glared at him.*
- *Leo and Danny were talking and Leo looked in his direction.*

> Go to p110 in your Workbook for help with your planning.

▶ **Contrast**
The writer uses *contrast*. He contrasts the characters of Danny and Leo.
Summarise in what way the two boys are different.
He contrasts how he felt before and after Leo came.
Summarise the writer's feelings before and after Leo came.

Writing assignment
You have read and discussed an autobiographical extract in which the writer remembers two people from his past. You are now going to write an autobiographical extract about a person / people who had an effect on you.

Study skills 3

Revision

> **What is revision?**
> **Revision** is going back over what you have learned in preparation for an exam.

There are lots of websites that give advice about how to revise. Look at these suggestions that students have made on a revision website.

make a timetable   **write short notes**

do practice papers   **begin revision early**

use mind maps   **revise with a friend**

summarise on index cards   **draw diagrams**

Activity

Have you used any of them? Which ones work for you?

Let's look at different things you can do to revise for your English exam.

1 Spelling

Begin with your own mistakes. Most of the vocabulary you will use in an exam will be vocabulary you have used before. Look back over your written work and list the words you have misspelled. Spend a little time each day learning these words.

- Use mnemonics.
  For example:
  Piece is commonly misspelled. Is it *ie* or *ei*? Just remember a p**ie**ce of p**ie**!
  Do I use *here* or *hear* (a sound)? Just remember you *hear* with your *ear*!
- Learn the rules for adding prefixes.
  If you add a prefix, the spelling of the root word DOES NOT change.
  For example: *appear / disappear   important / unimportant*
- Learn the rules for adding suffixes.
  If you add a suffix, sometimes the spelling of the root word DOES change.
  For example: *make / making   begin / beginning*
- Group words together that have the same spelling pattern and rhyme.
  For example: *flew   blew   drew   grew*

A **mnemonic** is something to help you remember.

Activity

Can you think of a good mnemonic to help you remember when to use:
there / their / they're and
were / where / we're?

Be careful with rules! There are usually some exceptions!

Activity

What words could you group together with the *ght* spelling pattern?

2 Grammar

All the grammar you need to learn is at the end of your Workbook in the Grammar Reference section. Look through it carefully and mark the sections you have most difficulty with. Spend some time learning, then ask a friend to test you.

Present simple   See English World 8 Units 1 and 4

1. We use the present simple for things that happen regularly.
   We *go* to the seaside every summer.   Joe *watches* TV every day.
2. There are some verbs which are normally only used in the simple form.
   I *know* that man.
   e.g. like, love, hate, want, understand, remember, need, prefer, know, mean, sound, think (have an opinion), have (possess)
3. We can use the present simple for fixed and certain events in the future.
   - Statements about the calendar: Today *is* Monday so tomorrow *is* Tuesday.
   - Events which cannot change: When *is* the next full moon?
   - Planned, fixed events: What time *is* the football match?
   - With verbs such as arrive, come, leave, start, etc, when referring to plans, programmes or schedules:
   Our train *leaves* in ten minutes.

Affirmative	I/You/We/They + verb	
	He/She/It + verb + s (or es)	They *take* exams once a year.
		John *plays* football every day.
		Sara *goes* to school by bus.

114 Study skills 3: revision

Comprehension

Comprehension is difficult to revise for because you do not know what the reading text is or what questions you will be asked.
You can, however, make sure you know the **types** of questions you will be asked.
Read this short text:

> John was looking out of the window. It was raining hard and a strong wind was blowing. He shivered and closed the window. His friends were playing in the street with a football but he didn't want to join in.

- **Question type 1 – Literal:** These are straightforward questions where you can find the exact words of the answer in the text, e.g.
  Question: What was John doing? **Answer:** He was looking out of the window.
- **Question type 2 – Inferential:** The text does not give you the answer to these questions directly. you have to look for clues, e.g.
  Question: How do you know John was cold? **Answer:** We know John was cold because it says 'he shivered'.
  This is not a literal question because the text doesn't say 'John was cold', e.g.
  Question: Why do you think John shivered? **Answer:** He shivered because the window was open.
- **Question type 3 – Personal response:** These questions are asking you for your opinion or what you would do, e.g. **Question:** Would you go out in the rain? Why? / Why not? **Answer:** I would / would not go out in the rain because …

> **Activity**
> Look through the comprehension exercises in your Student Book or practice papers. Discuss what type of questions are being asked.

Writing

- Correct spelling and grammar are very important parts of your writing but you should also revise the features of different writing styles.
- A good way to do this is to make a list of the different writing styles you have studied and the features / things you need to think about to include. Put each style on a small card, e.g.

Type:	Discursive essay [9 features]
Features:	subject
	writer's opinion
	purpose
	clear opening paragraph
	for and against arguments with reasons
	final paragraph – summary
	persuasive language
	appeal to readers
	facts
Useful words / phrases:	however / although / even though / for example / some people say / for this reason

> **Activity**
> For a discursive essay there are nine features. Cover the box. Can you name them?
> Work in pairs or groups. Choose a writing style and make a card like the one above. Share it with the class. Can they add anything you have missed?

Add useful words and phrases where appropriate.

WB p124

Project 1: Advertisements (Unit 1)

Create an advertisement page for a magazine.

The page can have:
- a single advertisement.
- two or more advertisements.

If you wish, you can create a double page with:
- one advertisement.
- more than one advertisement.

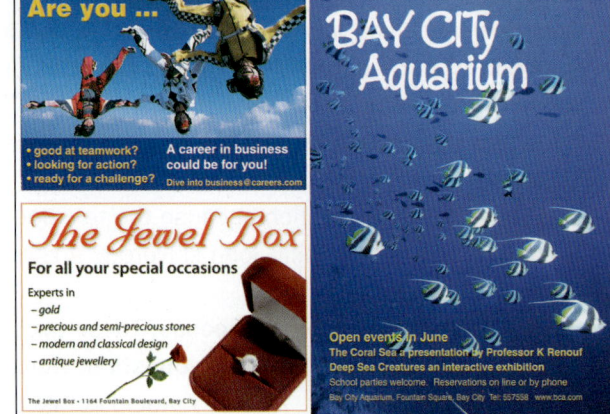

▶ **You can choose what is advertised. Here are some ideas.**

- a **product**, e.g. shoes, clothes, computers, cars
- a **service**, e.g. taxis, photocopying, dentist
- a **good cause**, e.g. environmental protection, a children's charity
- a **business**, e.g. car repairs, hairdresser, baker's
- an **event**, e.g. a concert, a public firework display

▶ **Remember to choose the words and pictures carefully.**

An advertisement can have:
- lots of words giving a lot of information.
- a few words.
- a picture and the brand name only.

The visual appearance of an advertisement is very important.

Look at advertisements in some magazines. Decide for yourself how effective they are.
Think about the right kind of picture or pictures for your own advertisement.
Look on the internet for images or draw your own.

▶ **Create your advertisement page with words and pictures. You can:**

- use a computer.
- draw and write everything yourself.
- add photos or other pictures.

Don't choose product names that actually exist – make up your own names.

Don't copy an advertisement that already exists – you can follow a style but you must create your own design.

Advertising is big business.
Companies spend a lot of money getting it right. Artists, photographers, designers and writers all come up with ideas and work together to create advertisements that people will notice.

Project 2: An entertainment review (Unit 4)

Choose a form of entertainment. Here are some ideas.

TV programme   film   music album   concert   theatre performance   computer game

- You can choose an informative TV programme, a drama, a game show or any other kind.
- The film can be one you saw in a cinema or on DVD.
- You can review any kind of performance or concert, including opera and classical music, and any kind of recorded music.

The important thing is that it is something you have seen or heard yourself.

Explain briefly what the programme, film, performance or game was about.

Explain briefly what kind of music you heard if you are reviewing a performance or recording.

> **Don't** review something you have not personally experienced.

> **Don't** write out the complete story.

> **Don't** explain each song or piece of music in detail.

Decide how good the entertainment was. Think about these as appropriate:

music   costumes   scenery

plot   actors   singing

photography   presenter

> **Don't** just say "It was good. I liked it" or "It was terrible. I didn't like it at all."

Remember
Your readers want to know your opinion.
Important! They want to know why. Give reasons.

… unrealistic scenery and the tree fell over twice.   … exciting because there were six car chases.

   … started with amazing fireworks …   … a ridiculous plot, nothing like real life.

   … wonderful, brightly coloured costumes.   … the music will stay in my head for ages …

   … two of the songs were boring and too long.   … full of interesting information …

Give the entertainment stars out of five or marks out of ten. Illustrate your review.

Project 3: A magazine travel feature (Unit 6)

A magazine feature can be two pages or several pages. A travel feature aims to interest readers in going to the places it mentions, finding out more about them or just reading the feature itself for interest.

Your feature can include:

- **information**
  – about different destinations

- a **travelogue**
  – a personal account of a visit to a destination

- **reviews**
  – of anything to do with travel: a hotel, a city, an air flight or train journey

- **advertisements** – for travel companies, hotels, cities, airlines or luggage

The sun-soaked, tropical islands of the West Indies are lapped by the azure Caribbean Sea …

… so a great way to see Paris is from the river and a boat trip on a summer evening is a great way to cool down, too.

Hotel Majestic ** The views are lovely but the small pool is crowded and it's a long walk to the beach.

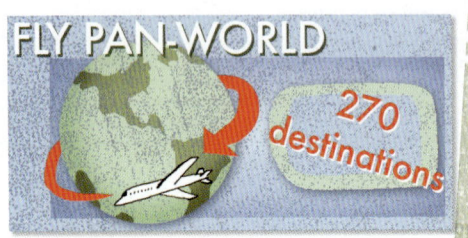

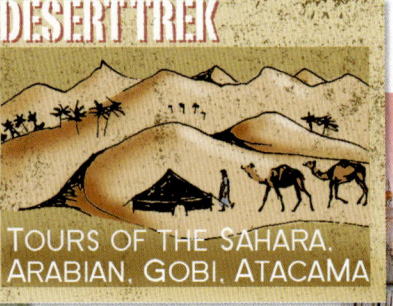

FLY PAN-WORLD
270 destinations

FREE HANDBAG WITH THIS SET OF SUITCASES

DESERT TREK
TOURS OF THE SAHARA, ARABIAN, GOBI, ATACAMA

Venice, city of dreams

You can include a variety of destinations and advertisements for places around the world or you can focus on particular destinations, such as great cities or wonderful mountain regions.

If you wish, you can choose just one country or city and write a complete feature on it: all the reviews and advertisements would also be about that one place.

Travel features usually have several photos. They catch the reader's attention and help to show what a place is like. The photos are usually very striking and attractive.

You can write a feature about a place or places you have been to yourself or you can choose a place that you have not been to. Find out about it. Imagine you have been there and write information, a personal account and reviews. Use the internet or magazines to give you ideas of places to write about.

Don't copy out text that was written by somebody else!

Do find out facts. Think and write your own ideas in your own words.

Project 4: An informative magazine article (Unit 8)

Choose a subject that interests you. It can be a popular subject or something that not many people know about. Here are some ideas but you can choose anything at all.

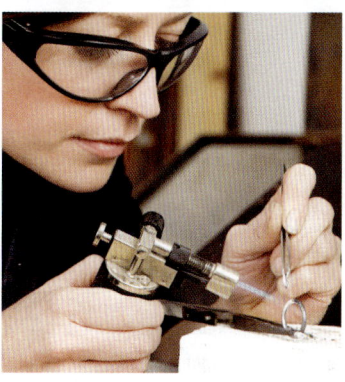

What you can include in the article

Your article can have different sections. You can include any or all of these:

- information
- interviews
- personal recount
- short biography

What do you know?

If you already know a lot about the subject, make notes about what you know. Decide if you need to find out more facts or more detail. Do more research if you need to.
If you only know a little, find out more and make notes, then research and make more notes.
If you choose a popular subject, try to add some new and different information that you find out yourself.

How to develop your ideas

Think about the notes and information you have. Decide what sections your article will have.
Use your notes to write the different sections.

Use accurate facts:
- to write clear information.
- to write a short biography.
- to write an explanation.

Use your imagination:
- to write an interview with somebody involved in your chosen subject.
- to write a personal recount of an event or experience connected with the subject.

Think about illustrations
- photos
- drawings
- maps

Think about design
- fonts
- colours
- borders
- boxes

Look back at some of the pages in this book to give you ideas.

Project 5: A magazine opinion page (Unit 9)

Create a magazine opinion page about an issue of your choice.

You can choose something of global significance such as climate change or environmental damage, or something that is important to you, your school or your neighbourhood.

Opinion pages include different opinions. You will need to write different opinions even if you don't agree with them. If you only have one view on a subject and cannot see any other point of view – choose something else!

Decide how you want to present the views about the issue you have chosen.

- You could write **emails** making different points.

I think that wearing a uniform in school gives a feeling of belonging together and …	I dislike looking the same as everyone else. We are all individuals so we should …

- You could write **interviews** with different people giving opposite points of view.

Interviewer: Why is tourism a problem? Environmentalist: In large numbers tourists damage the places they visit. Interviewer: How do they do that? Environmentalist: Hotels are built and they …	Hotel owner: Tourism is very important. Interviewer: In what ways? Hotel owner: Tourists bring in money and jobs are created in hotels and cafés. Interviewer: What about the damage to …?

- You could write **an article** that explains an issue and includes different opinions about it.

> Sport helps people to stay healthy but there are different views as to whether students should be forced …
> Some people say it is better if individuals choose for themselves whether to … because …
> The opposite view is that people don't always choose wisely, so it's better if …

Think about the subject. Note down all the different points that can be made about it. Make sure you have at least six. Choose how to present them. Write the views.

Illustrate the views with drawings or photos. Use two pages if you need to.

Project 6: A complete magazine

In projects 1–5 you wrote these magazine pages:
- an advertisement page
- a review
- a travel feature
- an informative article
- an opinion page

Now you can use them to create your own magazine.

In pairs or small groups up to four

Look at all your project work.
You could have up to 40 pages altogether.
Read each other's work.

In larger groups of five or more

Look at all your project work. Read each other's work and count the total number of pages.
Decide if you want to use all the pages or choose the best pages to make your magazine.
Aim to include at least 40 pages but not more than 60.

All groups

Decide on the best order for the pages. Look at other magazines to give you ideas.
Decide on a name for your magazine. Design a cover.
Check the pages are in the best order. Number them.
Write a contents page.
Fix the pages inside the cover.

Give a two-minute presentation of your magazine.
- Explain why you chose the title.
- Tell the other students some of the contents of your magazine.
- Show some of the pages.

Read each other's magazines.

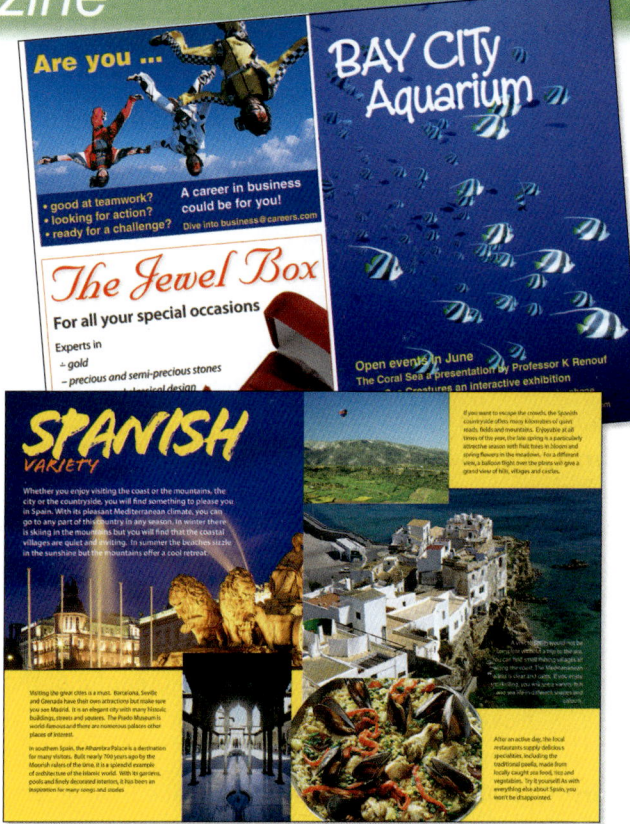

Optional

- Include stories. Write stories especially for your magazine or include the best fiction writing you have done during the year.
- Improve articles if you wish. Add more pictures or add complete picture pages with captions or a small amount of text.

Audio scripts for Conversation focus sections

Start-up

🎧 1.01

Unit 1, page 7

Scene: The school library.

Liam: Hi, Kurt, you're in school early! What are you reading?
Kurt: *The International Times* newspaper – the review page. I've got to write a review for my English project so I thought I'd look at a real one.
Liam: Let's see … well, that's not a review.
Kurt: No, it's an advert but it's more interesting than the review.
Liam: What's it for?
Kurt: It's asking people to give money.
Liam: You haven't got any money, have you?
Kurt: No, but my dad has. I think I'll show it to him. What are you doing here, anyway?
Liam: Oh, I'm just putting up this notice about the festival. Mia asked me to do it on my way to athletics practice.
Kurt: Oh, yes, you're in the 100-metre sprint final, next week, aren't you?
Liam: Mm, supposed to be. My time's dreadful at the moment. I think I need some new trainers. I need some for tennis, anyway. Are you coming to watch the match after school?
Kurt: I can't. I'm going to the dress rehearsal of *King Lear* in the hall.
Liam: You're not in it, are you?
Kurt: No, but I'm going to review it – that's why I'm looking at the review section, I told you.
Liam: Oh yes, so you did. Well, maybe see you at lunchtime.
Kurt: Definitely! We've got the student council meeting at lunchtime, remember?
Liam: Oh, right! What are we talking about?
Kurt: The festival, using the new language lab and litter.
Liam: Litter? We're always talking about litter.
Kurt: That's because it's always a problem.
Liam: Yes … Right … Well, see you later, then.
Kurt: OK, see you … and don't be late!

🎧 1.07

Unit 2, page 17

Scene: The school music department.

[Sound of Photocopier being used.]

Florence: Are you going to be long with the copier, Gustav?
Gustav: No, I've nearly finished.
Florence: What are you printing?
Gustav: The orchestra rehearsal schedule. Why don't you take your copy now?
Florence: OK, thanks.

[Running footsteps.]

Gustav: Hey, Giorgio! Walk in the corridor!
Giorgio: Sorry, Gustav.

[Footsteps slow and halt.]

Gustav: Here's your orchestra rehearsal schedule.
Giorgio: (*breathless*) OK, thanks, Gustav. Hmm, we've got a lot of rehearsals, haven't we?
Gustav: Of course, we have to be perfect.
Giorgio: Oh, look. Wednesday's rehearsal clashes with the jazz band.
Gustav: Jazz band?
Giorgio: Yes, I've just joined it, it's great. We're thinking of working something up for the festival.
Gustav: Jazz? At the festival?
Florence: Why not, Gustav? The committee is planning to include a professional jazz band in the festival programme, as well.
Gustav: Really?
Giorgio: And an indie band.
Gustav: A what?
Giorgio: You know, Gustav, a band that writes their own music to their own style. They've been in touch with a brilliant group, everyone loves them and lots of people will want to come and hear them. It'll be fantastic.
Gustav: You mean, a pop group, at the festival?
Giorgio: Well, kind of a pop group, yes.
Florence: I think it will be great to have lots of different kinds of music at the festival.
Giorgio: So do I. I'd really like to hear a great blues singer.
Florence: And a swing band.
Giorgio: Yes, terrific. And what about a folk group?
Gustav: Well, they won't have all that at the festival.
Florence: I think they might, Gustav. It won't just be Mozart, Schubert and Bach, you know.
Giorgio: That's right. They've been talking about having lots of different kinds of music.
Florence: They're meeting to finalise the programme tomorrow.
Gustav: Huh!

[Firm footsteps going away.]

Giorgio: Hey, Gustav, where are you going?
Gustav: (*receding voice*) To get my laptop, of course! This needs action!

Audio scripts for Conversation focus sections

Unit 3, page 29

Scene: The school hallway by the noticeboard.

[Sound of chairs being stacked.]

Florence: Look at that poster, Mimi. The film club is showing *West Side Story* next week.

Mimi: I've never seen *West Side Story*.

Florence: It's fantastic. It's one of my favourite musicals.

Mimi: It's based on a Shakespeare play, isn't it?

Florence: Yes, that's right. *Romeo and Juliet*.

Mimi: I've seen that on stage. It's so sad. From the start you know that Romeo and Juliet are going to die.

Florence: You still want to watch the play, though.

Mimi: Yes, of course. You get drawn into the story from the very first words.

Florence: That's the skill of an exceptional writer.

Mimi: I wonder if a Shakespeare play will be included in the festival.

Florence: I don't know. I don't think they've arranged the performance programme yet.

Mimi: I'm hoping they might invite a famous author to read and talk about writing.

Florence: That would be something new! We've never had a famous author visit the school.

Mimi: They'll need to find something really good to start the whole festival off.

Florence: I agree. If the start of the festival is good, people will want to come to lots of other events.

Mimi: They could begin with a huge concert.

Florence: Yes, they could. But not everyone likes classical music.

Mimi: True. What about a big brass band, then? Or massed choirs? Or a firework display?

Florence: They might start off with *The River Boys*.

Mimi: (enthusiastically) *The River Boys*? How do you know they're in the programme?

Florence: My sister Lucie told me. She's on the festival committee.

Mimi: Great! Their last concert started with an incredible drum solo – followed by a brilliant sound and light show. Magic!

Florence: Not everyone likes pop music, though.

Mimi: Hmm … What about … a firework display with a live orchestra … erm … playing Handel's Firework music! Followed by *The River Boys*' latest multi-media show with … er … a choral backing group and a hundred dancers in front of a specially created stage set?

Florence: (laughs) Sounds amazing! You ought to be on the committee, Mimi.

Mimi: Too right! I've got all the ideas.

[Bell rings.]

Florence: Oh, that's our break over. Come on, it's maths next.

Mimi: That's a pity. Thinking about the festival is much more fun!

Unit 4, page 39

Scene: The school hall.

Liam: Hey, Kurt! That was a big audience this evening!
Kurt: Yes, it was great. We nearly ran out of chairs.
Liam: I was surprised, weren't you?
Kurt: Not really. *West Side Story* is a well-known film with great music and fantastic performances.
Liam: And what amazing dancers! How do they move so fast?
Kurt: Practice, Liam, practice! Dancing is really hard work. Did you see the documentary on TV last night about students at the Cuban National Ballet? Their rehearsals looked really exhausting. Everything has to be perfect.
Liam: No, I didn't watch that. I prefer documentaries about events that are happening now.
Kurt: You mean current affairs?
Liam: Yes. I think it's important for people to know what's going on in the world.
Kurt: Yes, I agree, it's good to be well-informed. But some TV programmes only tell you one side of things, you know.
Liam: Yes, you're right. I watched a programme about exploring for oil. Really, it was so one-sided!
Kurt: Was it? Why?
Liam: It gave the impression there was no risk at all in drilling into any part of the Earth to find oil and that pollution is only a small problem. That's just not true.
Kurt: Hmm, yes, I can see that environmentalists might have a different view.
Liam: Absolutely! And there are some great documentary films about climate change and its effect on the environment.
Kurt: Yes, and some fantastic nature documentaries. You can watch animals that you'll never really see yourself – unless you become an explorer!
Liam: *(laughs)* That's true! What about showing one for film club?
Kurt: Maybe. Or we could suggest one for the arts festival. Tasha has asked us for ideas, remember?
Liam: Oh, yes.
Kurt: Gustav wants us to show a biographical documentary of Mozart because there's a whole concert of his music.
Liam: That's a great idea.
Kurt: Perhaps we could show a series of different documentary films, as well as some feature films. What do you think?
Liam: Sounds great to me. Let's get back to Tasha and see what she thinks.

🎧 1.19

Unit 5, page 51

Scene: The classroom.

Giorgio: What are you going to volunteer for, Florence?
Florence: I'd like to help with refreshments. What about you?
Giorgio: Meeting and greeting people, I think. It'll be more fun and less hard work.
Florence: Really, Giorgio, you're not supposed to think about it like that!
Giorgio: Why not? Isn't it a good idea to choose what you enjoy doing?
Florence: Well, yes … but … Oh, well, I suppose you've got a point.
Giorgio: Look, there's going to be a talent evening. Are you going to audition for that?
Florence: No. Gustav is going to audition. He's much better than me. They won't choose two violinists.
Giorgio: How do you know? They might.
Florence: You've forgotten that my sister Lucie's on the committee. She said they want a variety of performers for the talent evening not just loads of classical musicians.
Giorgio: Hah! Better not tell Gustav that.
Florence: He already knows. They discussed it in the committee and then they discussed it with Gustav. He agrees.
Giorgio: That's a surprise. How did they persuade him?
Florence: It wasn't difficult. They booked his uncle's orchestra. Gustav could see that classical music would be significant in the festival. After that, he was fine about other music and performers being in the programme. And in the talent evening.
Giorgio: He isn't on the committee, though.
Florence: No, but he's important in the musical life of the school and he works hard at it. Much better to have him supporting the music programme than fighting against it.
Giorgio: It was very skilful work by the committee.
Florence: I agree. They listened to what Gustav had to say and looked at all sides of the issue, then came up with a solution that worked for everyone.
Giorgio: You make the committee's work sound easy.
Florence: Well, it is when it goes right.
Giorgio: And when it doesn't?
Florence: They ask for advice, of course. Mr Simpson has been helping them a lot. Don't you ask for advice when you have a problem?
Giorgio: Yes, of course. I talk to my mum and dad, usually. What about you?
Florence: I often talk to Lucie. She's good at listening and finding solutions.
Giorgio: I expect that's why she's on the committee. You'd be good on a committee, too.
Florence: Well, I'm not sure I have all the necessary qualities.
Giorgio: Of course you have, Florence. Anyway, let's fill in these forms.
Florence: Good idea. We can hand them in on our way to orchestra practice.

Unit 6, page 61
Scene: The school library.

[Liam is online, so we can hear him typing.]

Liam: Fantastic! I've found the blog of Professor Barnes' dig in Scotland.
Kurt: Oh?
Liam: Yeah … He's coming here, you know.
Kurt: Is he?
Liam: Yes, for the festival, remember? He's going to give a talk about … Kurt, are you listening?
Kurt: Yes, sorry, Liam. I was looking at these photos of the Atacama Desert.
Liam: The Atacama Desert? Where's that?
Kurt: South America.
Liam: Let's have a look … Hmm. There doesn't seem to be anything there.
Kurt: Well, there isn't. That's the point. The air is clean and clear. It's a good place for special telescopes and there is a huge one there. In the desert. I'd like to go and see it.
Liam: Really? I'd prefer to go to Scotland. I want to visit the excavations. They've found an ancient royal palace, you know. Perhaps I could volunteer to work on the dig.
Kurt: Ugh. It's always cold and wet in Scotland.
Liam: Not always. Anyway, I'm from Ireland so I'm used to it. Hello, Mimi.
Mimi: Hi, Liam. Hello, Kurt. Could you put this poster on the notice board for me? I can't quite reach.
Kurt: Of course. What's it about?
Mimi: Eliza Brodie's new book. It's being published just before the festival and she's coming to talk about it.
Kurt: What's it called?
Mimi: *Himalayan Adventure*. It's set in the Himalayan mountains, you see.
Liam: Aha! That makes sense!
Mimi: Yes, of course. It's such a dramatic place for a story. I'd love to go there and see where it all happens, wouldn't you?
Liam: Err … no.
Mimi: *(surprised)* No? Why ever not?
Liam: Too much effort. All that walking uphill.
Mimi: You're so lazy, Liam! What about you, Kurt?
Liam: It's no good asking him. He's off to the Atacama Desert.
Mimi: The Atacama? How interesting!
Kurt: Yes, but the Himalayas sound interesting, too.
Mimi: Oh, they are. And you must come and hear Eliza Brodie talk about her book.
Kurt: Of course, Mimi. It sounds great.
Liam: We wouldn't miss it for anything!
Mimi: *(pauses)* Hmm. See you later, anyway.
Kurt: Bye, Mimi.

[Footsteps going away.]

You're such a tease, Liam.
Liam: Me? What did I say?

2.05

Unit 7, page 73

Scene: At the end of the school orchestra practice.

[Sounds of last few bars of school orchestra rehearsal.]

Gustav: Excellent! A great rehearsal everyone, well done.

[Sounds of everyone putting away instruments and chairs.]

Giorgio: Thanks, Gustav. See you next week.

Gustav: No, tomorrow, Giorgio. We've got extra rehearsals for *Romeo and Juliet*.

Giorgio: *Romeo and Juliet*? That's a play by Shakespeare! We're not doing a play.

Florence: You've forgotten, Giorgio, the film club is showing *Romeo and Juliet* at the festival. And we're going to perform some music from the soundtrack before it starts.

Gustav: Of course, the music for the film was not written by a classical composer.

Florence: *(sigh)* No, but it's lovely music, Gustav, and I'm sure everyone will enjoy it.

Gustav: Well, perhaps.

Florence: Anyway, it's a really good film. I used to think Shakespeare's plays were boring. Then I saw this film and it really changed my mind. It all comes alive when you watch actors playing the parts.

Giorgio: That's true. I didn't like books by Charles Dickens. Then I saw the film of *Oliver Twist* and I really liked it.

Florence: I've seen that, too. It made me want to read some more books by Dickens.

Gustav: Ah, good. Classic fiction should be read. Just watching the film is too easy.

Florence: Well, it's a different experience, isn't it?

Gustav: Shakespeare's work should be performed, of course. But Dickens wrote novels for people to read.

Florence: Yes, but he performed dramatic readings from his novels. Did you know that, Gustav? He used to read aloud and play all the characters himself.

Gustav: Yes, I did know that, of course. But he read all the narrative as well, you know, and his wonderful descriptions. It's important to read those, too.

Florence: I agree with you, Gustav. But if people become interested in reading classic fiction because they see a film or watch it on TV, I think that's a good thing.

Giorgio: I do, too. I saw one of Eliza Brodie's books as a TV film. Fantastic! I've read all her books now.

Gustav: But she's not a classic writer, Giorgio.

Giorgio: She might be one day, Gustav. Like *The River Boys* might be classic musicians.

Gustav: *(snorts)* I doubt it.

Giorgio: I thought you'd decided you like them, Gustav. You've bought a ticket for their concert, haven't you?

Gustav: Well, I'm going to see them but it doesn't mean they're classic ... or even good!

Florence: No, but it might mean that you enjoy them.

Gustav: *(snorts)* We'll see about that.

Giorgio: Come on, Gustav, I bet you end up dancing wildly like everyone else.

Gustav: *(snorts)* I can't imagine that!

Florence and Giorgio: Hmm ...

2.09
Unit 8, page 83
Scene: the school library.

[Sound of keyboard being used slowly.]
[Footsteps approach.]

Mimi: Oh, hello, Kurt, could I use the computer? I want to search the library catalogue. I'll be quick.

Kurt: Oh, OK. You can use it now, Mimi. I was just checking for the instructions on how to use the whiteboard.

Mimi: The interactive whiteboard?

Kurt: Yes, that's right. I've got to do a presentation of my art project.

Mimi: We haven't used the whiteboard yet. It looks amazing. How does it work?

Kurt: How does it work? I've no idea! I just want to use it. But I don't understand it!

Mimi: Well, I don't understand my science project, so I want to find a book about it.

[Sound of keyboard being used quickly.]

Kurt: What do you need to find out about?

Mimi: Electricity. I'd rather find out about keyhole surgery but it's electricity this term. Florence and I are doing a project together. Do you know about electricity, Kurt?

Kurt: No, not a lot. Why don't you just look online?

Mimi: We did but there wasn't enough detail. Ah, here's the book we need. I'll go and look for it.

[Footsteps going away.]
[Sound of keyboard being used slowly.]
[Footsteps approach.]

Florence: Hi, Kurt, do you mind if I use the computer? I …

Kurt: Don't tell me, Florence, you've got a science project.

Florence: How did you know?

Kurt: Mimi was just here. Electricity is it?

Florence: No, well, yes, … but I want to find out about carbon dating.

Kurt: *(surprised)* Carbon dating? What do you want to know about that for?

Florence: Professor Barnes has discovered an ancient royal palace in Scotland. He's using carbon dating to find out how old the site is. I want to know how it works. I've looked it up online but …

Kurt: *(interrupting)* There wasn't enough detail.

Florence: That's right. *(pauses)* How did you know?

Kurt: Never mind.

[Sound of keyboard being used quickly.]

Florence: Ah, here's the book I need.

[Footsteps approach.]

Mimi: It's OK, Florence, I've already got the book on electricity.

Florence: Great! I just want to get this book on carbon dating. I won't be a moment.

[Footsteps going away.]

Mimi: So have you understood the instructions for the whiteboard, Kurt?

Kurt: No, not yet. I had just found them when you arrived, as a matter of fact.

[Footsteps approach.]

Florence: OK, Mimi. I've got the book I wanted. Let's go.

Mimi: You'd better hurry up, Kurt. The bell for the next lesson will go in a moment.

Florence and Mimi: Bye Kurt!

[Footsteps going away.]
[Sound of keyboard being used slowly.]

Kurt: Goodbye, girls! *(sigh)* Now, then …

[School bell rings.]

Kurt: Ugh!

2.13

Unit 9, page 95
Scene: The school computer room.

[Sound of photocopier being used.]

Liam:	Hi, Florence. Can I use the photocopier?
Florence:	I'm not using it, Liam.
Liam:	OK, thanks … Hey, you've left this sheet of paper in the photocopier, though.
Florence:	It's not mine.
Liam:	It's got your name on it – Duval, look.
Florence:	Let's see. Oh, it's Lucie's. It's the arrangements for the disabled children at the festival concert.
Liam:	You mean some children are coming who can't walk?
Florence:	Yes, that's right. They use wheelchairs. They each have a volunteer with them.
Liam:	Really? Why?
Florence:	In case there's a fire or something and everyone has to leave the hall. The volunteers have to know how to get the children out quickly. They've got a practice at lunchtime tomorrow.
Liam:	It seems like a lot of trouble to go to.
Florence:	*(challenging)* Do you think so? *(firmly)* If it means they can come to the concert, I don't think it's much trouble at all.
Liam:	OK, OK! You're very sure about it.
Florence:	I am. We've got a disabled cousin in France, you see. So I think equal opportunities are important. Isn't there anything that's important to you?
Liam:	Yes, of course.
Florence:	Like what?
Liam:	Well … animal rights.
Florence:	Animal rights?
Liam:	Yes. You know. Treating animals well. Not hurting them in scientific experiments, for example.
Florence:	I see. Don't you think people are more important?
Liam:	People can speak for themselves. When did you last hear a horse complain at being hit?
Florence:	I take your point. All the same, some people don't have much of a voice.
Liam:	How do you mean?
Florence:	Poor people, for instance. Who takes any notice of them?
Liam:	That's true. Lots of poor farmers have no land to work on because it's been sold to food companies who use machines.
Florence:	So the farmers get poorer still.
Liam:	Correct. And the poorest people are most affected by climate change. Now that really is important.
Florence:	I agree. It's going to be a big problem over the next century.
Liam:	It's one that we'll have to solve.

[School bell rings.]

Florence:	Yes, but not before the next lesson, though, Liam. I've got to go.
Liam:	OK. Nice talking to you, Florence.
Florence:	And you, Liam. I enjoy a good discussion. See you later.

Unit 10, page 105
Scene: The school café.

[Sounds of people chatting.]

Florence: Hasn't it been a great week so far, Mimi?
Mimi: Fantastic. The Egyptian art was my favourite thing up to now.
Florence: Oh, mine, too. It was such an interesting talk and the professor is so knowledgeable.
Mimi: And he's such a good presenter. He made everything so interesting, even a dusty, old stone!
Liam: Hiya, girls! Who's a dusty, old stone?
Mimi: Nobody is, Liam, don't be silly.
Florence: You're looking pleased with yourself.
Liam: I've got Professor Barnes to sign my copy of his book on Egyptian Art.
Mimi: Oo, I want one, too!
Liam: He's signing again after lunch in the library.
Mimi: I'll be there. Didn't you think he was amazing?
Liam: Of course. But I knew he would be. I think his work is inspiring. I've been following the dig in Scotland. I might be able to volunteer to work there during the summer.
Florence: Lucky you. Is this going to be your career, Liam?
Liam: Maybe. The more I see of Professor Barnes, the more interested in archaeology I get.
Kurt: Hi, Liam, can you move over?
Liam: Sure, Kurt. What've you got there?
Kurt: My photos of the sculptures. I want to include them in my art project.
Liam: Good idea to take your pictures before they disappear again!
Kurt: Yes, that was a bit of a panic, wasn't it?
Liam: A good thing Miss Jackson never panics.
Mimi: No, she's a great person to have around in a crisis.
Florence: She's really helped the committee and I know they all look up to her.
Mimi: Hey, those are really good photos, Kurt.
Kurt: Thanks, but have you seen Lucie's? They're even better.
Mimi: Yes, she showed them to us.
Kurt: She's putting them in her portfolio for art college, you know.
Liam: I'm sure she'll get in. She's a brilliant photographer.
Florence: She always likes to get things exactly right.
Mimi: So do you, Florence.
Florence: Well, I try to follow Lucie's example.
Gustav: Hello, everyone!
All: Hi, Gustav!
Gustav: Look what I've got. It's the recording of our Mozart concert. It's marvellous. I'll play it to you. The sound quality is fantastic.

[Footsteps approaching.]

Giorgio: Hey, Gustav. Can I play my recording of the jazz band on your player? Please, please? I've just got it and I want Florence to hear her solo.
Gustav: *(shocked)* Jazz solo, Florence, on a violin!?
Florence: Erm …
Gustav: *(tuts)* I was just about to play some Mozart, Giorgio. Oh, well, if you must, here you are.
Giorgio: Thanks, Gustav. I'll just take this other disc out – oh, it's the River Boys' CD.
Florence: Gustav! Did you buy the River Boys' CD?
Gustav: Yes … well … I decided they were quite good, after all.
Florence, Mimi: *(surprised)* Gustav!
Giorgio: Did you really, Gustav?
Gustav: Yes … Well … Quite good, I said … But not a patch on Mozart, of course!
All: Oh, Gustav!

... and finally

You have read or written about everything in these photos in studying *English World*. Read the list. Number the photos.

How well do you know the world? On the map on pages 134 – 135, write the number of the photo next to the correct numbered location.

1 Switzerland
2 Grand Canyon
3 koala bear
4 Taj Mahal
5 Giant's Causeway
6 Blue Mosque
7 Winter Palace
8 Great Wall
9 coral
10 St Basil's Cathedral
11 Alaskan coast
12 Nile
13 Thames
14 Pyramids
15 Uluru
16 Ben Nevis
17 Mount Everest
18 Beijing
19 London Eye
20 Hong Kong harbour
21 Sydney harbour
22 Japanese coast
23 polar bear
24 Chrysler building
25 Niagara Falls
26 Amazon
27 Eiffel Tower
28 Alhambra Palace
29 Masai Mara national park
30 Grand Palace

132 ... and finally

... and finally 133

Find the location of the photos from pages 132 and 133. Write the numbers on the map.

- ㉕ The Arctic
- Greenland
- Alaska
- ㉔ Alaska Coast
- Canada
- Vancouver
- Quebec
- Montreal
- ㉓ Niagara Falls
- ㉑ New York
- North America
- ㉒ Colorado Grand Canyon Arizona
- Atlantic Ocean
- Pacific Ocean
- Manaus
- ㉖ Brazil
- South America
- Rio

134 ... and finally

Ocean

Norway
⑧ St Petersburg
Asia
Russia
⑨ Moscow
• Samara
UK
Berlin
London Germany Poland
④ Prague
① Switzerland Czech Republic
Paris ③ Austria Vienna
France Milan Europe
Italy
⑩
Istanbul • Ankara
Turkey
Lebanon
• Amman Beijing
Cairo Jordan ⑲ ⑰
Giza ⑫ Himalayas China Japan
Africa Egypt Dubai Delhi ⑳
• ⑮
United Arab Jaipur Hong Kong
Emirates • ⑱
⑭
India
⑪ Thailand
Bangkok
⑯

Kenya
⑬
• Thika Indian Ocean
Nairobi

Coast of NE Australia
Queensland ㉗
㉙ Great Barrier
Uluru Reef
Johannesburg Australia Brisbane •
S Australia
South Africa ㉚ New South Wales
Sydney ㉘

...and finally 135

Macmillan Education
Between Towns Road, Oxford OX4 3PP
A division of Macmillan Publishers Limited

Companies and representatives throughout the world

ISBN 978-0-230-03254-5

Text © Liz Hocking, Wendy Wren, Mary Bowen 2013
Design and illustration © Macmillan Publishers Limited 2013

The authors have asserted their right to be identified as the authors of this work in accordance with the Copyright, Design and Patents Act 1988

First published 2013

All rights reserved; no part of this publication may be reproduced, stored in a retrieval system, transmitted in any form, or by any means, electronic, mechanical, photocopying, recording, or otherwise, without the prior written permission of the publishers.

Concept design by Anna Stasinska
Page design, layout and art editing by Wild Apple Design Ltd
Illustrated by Martin Bustamante (Advocate) pp84, 85, 88, 91. Kay Dixey (Graham Cameron) pp74, 75, 76, 77, 81, 106, 107, 108, 109, 119. Niall Harding (Beehive Illustration) pp30, 31, 32, 33, 34, 42, 52, 53, 54, 55, 59. Kate Rochester (Pickled Ink) pp12, 14, 35, 44, 66, 78, 90, 118. Mark Ruffle pp8, 25.

Cover design by Oliver Design Ltd
Cover Credit: Macmillan Dictionary, Rex Features/Upperhall Ltd/Robert Harding, Rex Features /Burger/Phanie, STOCKBYTE.
Picture research by Victoria Townsley-Gaunt

The publishers would like to thank the Macmillan teams around the world and Hala Fouad, Hoda Garraya, Caroline Toubia, Samira Maharneh, Adnan Bazbaz, Nisreen Attiya, Mohammed Abu Wafa, Fatima Saleh, Muna Ghazi, Anna Solovyeva, Tatyana Olshevskaya, Irina Shikyants, Irina Burdun, Elena Mitronova, Inna Daugavet, Olga Pavlenko, Svetlana Potanina, Irina Ostrovskaya, Zhanna Suvorova, Sergey Kozlov, Olga Matsuk, Elena Gordeeva, Marina Kuznetsova.

The author and publishers would like to thank the following for permission to reproduce their photographs:

Alamy/Marc Anderson p11, Alamy/Lordprice Collection, p102(cr), Alamy/dbimages p94(tl), Alamy/Mary Evans Picture Library p72(tr), Alamy/Corbis Flirt p117(concert), Alamy/LOOK Die Bildagentur der Fotografen GmbH p17(wing), Alamy/Paul Glendell p119(br), Alamy/David J. Green p119(bl), Alamy/Dennis Hallinan p91, Alamy/Blaine Harrington III p118(bmr), Alamy/Arcaid Images p102(cmll), Alamy/James Jackson p102(tcr), Alamy/MBI p68(2l), Alamy/Rod McLean p132(tm), Alamy/Moodboard p13(tr), Alamy/Dave Pattison p18(t), Alamy/Photo 12 p9(br), Alamy/PhotoAlto sas p7(tl), Alamy/Science Photo Library p51(cr), Alamy/Roman Milert p94(tr), Alamy/Muskopf Photography, LLC p68(2l), Alamy/NASA p87, Alamy/Dennis Sabo pp40, 42, Alamy/BlueMoon Stock p8; Alamy/Stockbroker p117(game), Alamy/Tony West p16(t); **Bananastock** pp26, 71, 104(cl), 116(sofa), 132(bcm); **Brand X Pictures** pp19(b), 20(b), 35(laptop), 116(sofa, Florence, Pisa), 21(Buckingham Palace, Palace) 123(b), 132(bcr); **Corbis** pp7(br), 50(tl), 89(tr), 104(tr, tl), 116(world, boats), 133(ctr, cm) 132(cm, cr, br), Corbis/Hasse Bengtsson/Johnér Images p99(mr) Corbis/Heide Benser p65, Corbis/Guy Ferrandis/Tristar Pictures/Bureau L.A. Collection p105(cl), Corbis/Rana Faure p4(tmr), Corbis/Vladimir Godnik/moodboard p45(t), Corbis/George Hammerstein p9(l), Corbis/Andrew McConnell/Robert Harding World p102(cl), Corbis/Dieter Heinemann/Westend61 p95(cr), Corbis/Edith Held p83(tl), Corbis/Saed Hindash/Star Ledger p38(tr), Corbis/Tetra Images p68(4l), Corbis/62° Nord/Johnér Images p5(Marit), Corbis/Erik Isakson p17(pop), Corbis/Chen Kai/Xinhua Press p29(t), Corbis/Serge Kozak p50(tl), Corbis/Yi Lu p118(bml), Corbis/Robert McGouey/All Canada Photos p9(r), Corbis/Camille Moirenc/Hemis p118(br), Corbis/Ocean pp13(br), 36, 89(cl), Corbis/Tim Pannell p13(tl), Corbis/Jose Luis Pelaez, Inc./Blend Images p7(tr), Corbis/Joel Rogers p63(b), 64(b), Corbis/Construction Photography p119(bl), Corbis/Richard Schultz p21(t), Corbis/Maria Schriber/Image Source p101(cr), Corbis/Charles Smith p95(tl), Corbis/Lawton/SoFood p89(cr), Corbis/Image Source pp47, 68(3l), Corbis/Hugh Sitton p118(bl), Corbis/Holger Spiering/Westend61 p38(background), Corbis/Mike Theiss/Ultimate Chase p38(cl); **Creatas** pp48(t), 116(Siena) 121(fountain); **Design Pics** p119(tl); **DigitalStock**/Corbis p132(ctr, tcm, cl); **Digital Vision** pp10(t), 56, 121(football); **Getty Images** p82(tr), 116(yo-yo, skydiving, rose) 119(tr, bml), 121(basketball, rubbish), 122, 123(t), 124(b), 129, 133(cl), 58(t), 105(cr, b) 118(cr), Getty Images/AFP pp84(background), 86(tr), 119(ml), Getty Images/Bloomberg p82(cl), Getty Images/Lars Borges p101(br), Getty Images/Rudi Von Briel p102(cmrr), Getty Images/Michael Blann pp18(br, bl), 20(t), p23(cm), Getty Images/Reggie Casagrande p116(br), Getty Images/Matthias Clamer p117(br), Getty Images/Kathy Collins pp9(m), p10(b), Getty Images/VisitBritain/Joe Cornish p132(tl), Getty Images/Cover p39(tr), Getty Images/James Darell p5(Zafira), Getty Images/Winston Davidian p61(female), Getty Images/Sylwia Duda p69, Getty Images/Melissa Farlow p60(tl), Getty Images/FBP p99(m), Getty Images/Robert Frerck p63(t), Getty Images/Fuse pp4(tl), 51(t), Getty Images/Tim Graham Photo Library p95(bl), Getty Images/Matt Henry Gunther p119(tr), Getty Images/Gavin Hellier

Robert Harding p60(cr), Getty Images/PT Images p68(1l), Getty Images/Flight Images LLP p103, Getty Images/Sean Justice p5(Lee), Getty Images/Tim Kitchen p99(r), Getty Images/David Lazar p119(tmr), Getty Images/Ron Levine pp4(tml), 5(Eva), 62(tr), Getty Images/David Malan p4(bl), Getty Images/Patti McConville p5(Liam), Getty Images/Dana Neely p83(cr), Getty Images/Philip Nealey p4(tl), Getty Images/Brand New Images p46, Getty Images/OMG p68(r), Getty Images/Nico De Pasquale Photography p16(cr), Getty Images/Yasinuss Photography pp62(cr), 64(cr), Getty Images/Science Photo Library p68(1r), Getty Images/Purestock p6(tr), Getty Images/Redferns pp17(traditional), 67(t), Getty Images/RAYMOND ROIG p39(cr), Getty Images/rubberball p50(tr), Getty Images/Christine Schneider/Brigitte p5(Giorgio), Getty Images/Alvis Upitis p16(cr), Getty Images/Travelstock44 - Juergen Held p61(tr), Getty Images/Visuals Unlimited, Inc./Gregory Basco p119(tl), Getty Images/Nick White pp13(bl), 67(b), Getty Images/Barry Winiker p4(background); Getty Images/Rainer Martini/LOOK-foto pp62(t), 64(t); **Glow images**/Rainer Martini/LOOK-foto pp62(t), 64(t); **Goodshot** pp116(Rome), 119(tm), 121(Bridge, Big Ben, Spain), 131, 133(tr, ctl), 132(cml); **Grapheast** pp61(cr, br); **The Henry Moore Foundation** p58(br); **Imagesource** pp6(tl), 48(b), 99(m), 116(Tuscany, fish) 121(dance, paella, balloons), 127(b), 133(bm, br, tm, tl, bl) 132(br, bl, bcl); **Istock** p121(gir); **JON FOXX IMAGES** p130; **Macmillan** p116(ducks), p133(bcr); **MACMILLAN AUSTRALIA** p104(bl), p133(bm), p132(cm); **Macmillan Dictionary** p110; **Macmillan Publishers Ltd**/Becoming Bindy, Jaclyn Moriarty p79(cl), Macmillan Publishers Ltd/Aurora/Julie Bertagna p79(cr), Macmillan Publishers Ltd/Michael Bourne, Brian Dyde, Nick Gillard and G.W. Lennox p60(bl), Macmillan Publishers Ltd/Verdigris Deep/Francis Hardinge p79(br), Macmillan Publishers Ltd/Gullstruck Island/Francis Hardinge p80(tr), Macmillan Publishers Ltd/Heroes and Villains/Anthony Horowitz p79(tl), Macmillan Publishers Ltd/Twilight Robbery/Francis Hardinge p79(bl), Macmillan Publishers Ltd/The Rekoning/James Jauncey p80(bmr), Macmillan Publishers Ltd/Young Sherlock Holmes Firestorm/Andrew Lane p79(tr), Macmillan Publishers Ltd/Young Sherlock Holmes. Death Cloud/Andrew Lane p80(br), Macmillan Publishers Ltd/Young Sherlock Holmes Black Ice/Andrew Lane p79(tr), Macmillan Publishers Ltd/Fated/Alison Noel p80(tl), Macmillan Publishers Ltd/Night Star/Alison Noel p80(bl), Macmillan Publishers Ltd/Paul Bricknell/Dean Ryan p15(t), Macmillan Publishers Ltd/Dragon Moon/Carole Wilkinson p80(bml); **Mary Evans**/AISA Media p57; **MEDIO IMAGES** p118(t); **National Geographic** p60(tr); **NASA** pp84(l), 86(br), **Photodisc** pp39(cl), 51(br), 96, 97, 98, 100, 116(ring), 126, 133(bcl); **Pixal** p61(forest); **Rex Features**/Everett Collection pp28(bl), 73(cr), Rex Features/Donald Cooper p72(tl), Rex Features/Columbia/Everett p72(tl), Rex Features/New Line/Everett p29(tl), Rex Features/W.Disney/Everett pp73(tr), 128, Rex Features/Upperhall Ltd/Robert Harding p102(tr), Rex Features/ITV p117(film), Rex Features/Kommersant Photo Agency p29(cr), Rex Features/Steve Meddle p117(TV programme), Rex Features/Alastair Muir p117(theatre), Rex Features/Image Source p60(cl), Rex Features/OJO Images p43, Rex Features /Burger/Phanie p27, Rex Features/Tim Rooke p3(br), Rex Features/Sipa Press p82(bl), Rex Features/SNAP p28(tl), Rex Features/Image Source p83(cl), Rex Features/WestEnd61 p89(b); **RSPCA PhotoLibrary** p94(cl); **Rubber Ball** p117(cm); **Science Photo Library**/NASA p119(bm); **Stockbyte** p6(bl), 127(t); **Superstock** p132(tr), SuperStock/AbleImages p105(t), SuperStock/Clover p111, SuperStock/Corbis p117(cl), SuperStock/Cusp p23(tr), SuperStock/Science Faction p83(tr), Superstock/Age Fotostock p112, SuperStock/Imagebroker.net p17(folk), SuperStock/Blend Images p6(cl), SuperStock/Tetra Images pp4(bml, br), SuperStock/Belinda Images pp45(b), 100(t), SuperStock/Ambient Images Inc.p102(cmr), Superstock/Culture Limited p5(Kurt), SuperStock/Mood board p17(jazz), SuperStock/Design Pics pp5(Miss Jackson), 24, Superstock/m Publishing p15(b), SuperStock/DreamPictures/Shannon Faulk /Purestock p5(Mimi), SuperStock/Kris Ubach/Quim Roser/age fotostock p99(l), SuperStock/SOMOS pp50(cl), 68(3r), SuperStock/Stockbroker p89(tl), SuperStock/Yuri Arcurs Media /SuperFusion p83(br), Superstock/Westend61 pp4(bmr), 7(cr); **Victoria and Albert Museum, London** pp102(br, cml); **Walker Books Ltd**/Antony Horowitz p28(tr); **Wateraid.org** p39(br).

The authors and publishers are grateful for permission to reprint the following copyright material:

Material from 'Z for Zachariah' by Robert C. O'Brien, copyright © Robert C. O'Brien 1998, reprinted by permission of Penguin Books UK; Material from WAR AND PEACE by Leo Tolstoy, translated by Anthony Briggs (Penguin Classics 2005, 2007). Translation Copyright © Anthony Briggs, 2005, reprinted by permission of the publisher; Quotation from 'Lord of the Rings' by J.R.R.Tolkien 1968, published by George Allen & Unwin Limited 1968; Text © 2000 Anthony Horowitz. Extract from STORMBREAKER written by Anthony Horowitz. Reproduced by permission of Walker Books Ltd, London SE11 5HJ.www.walker.co.uk

These materials may contain links for third party websites. We have no control over, and are not responsible for, the contents of such third party websites. Please use care when accessing them.

Although we have tried to trace and contact copyright holders before publication, in some cases this has not been possible. If contacted we will be pleased to rectify any errors or omissions at the earliest opportunity.

Printed and bound in Malaysia

2018 2017 2016 2015 2014 2013
10 9 8 7 6 5 4 3 2 1